CW00431669

PROLOGUE

Ask me where I was on 14th July 2016 and I'll answer without hesitation. I was at home, right there in front of the screen as we all were. Agog, disbelieving, and glued to the action. Texting friends and imploring them to watch.

"Can you believe it? I can't believe it. It's unbelievable isn't it?"

We couldn't believe it.

I, a thirty-nine-year-old man, leaping and frantic, was screaming at Chris Froome: "Ruuuuunnn! Find a bike. What's happened? This isn't fair. It isn't FAIR! They have to stop the race. Just ruuuuunnn...run FASTER!"

It was the Tour de France on Bastille Day. The stage was Mont Ventoux, the Giant of Provence, and the occasion was a big, bruising, bully of a bike race. The slopes of this massive slab were hosting the carnival atmosphere which accompanies (no, which *IS*) the Tour de France.

Tens of thousands of flag-waving-bike-chasing fans had gathered, and closed in, and stifled the procession of bikes and motorbikes on their slow drag up the mountain. Exuberance had tipped over into mild disorder. Chaos was descending.

The Grand Tour Diaries 2018

Pro cycling tales of mountains and mileage

Pete Linsley

(www.road-theory.com)

In my mind I pedal like Fignon...

Chris Froome had crashed into a motorbike in the melee and was now running up the mountain. *Running*. All clippy-cloppy in cycling shoes and Lycra. His rivals were further up the road and still in possession of their bikes and their senses. Froome had mislaid both. It wasn't fair, but *by God* it was great TV.

***

A Grand Tour, even a very normal one, is an extreme endeavour. A three-week race of three-thousand kilometres. Up mountain, down valley, crossing sun-baked plains and snow-ploughed passes. Benign one day and brutal the next. Skirting towns and criss-crossing cities. In and out of every cheap hotel from Paris, to Madrid, via Rome. It's the ultimate test for a pro cyclist.

Each start list is dotted with five, maybe six men who can win, while several-dozen of the world's fittest athletes form a supporting cast of gregarios and domestiques; servants to their leader's cause.

There's the Giro d'Italia; high-pitched and frantic, the (self-styled) Most Beautiful Race in the Most Beautiful Place. In high summer comes the Tour de France; a blockbuster TV spectacular of plot and sub-plot, sunflowers and champagne. And finally the Vuelta Espana, in September; sun-baked, lizard hot, and studded with steep Tarmac.

It was said, and is buried deep in the folklore of cycling, that each Grand Tour ridden shortens a man's life by a year. That the physical exertion required will literally, slowly, kill you.

Whatever the truth of that (and, let's be honest, there's poetic license at work), for a pro cyclist to ride one Grand Tour in a year is doable, and to ride two is tough. Three is rare. For many, the completion of *any* Grand Tour at *any* time is an achievement.

But what of we mere mortals? Assuming the Grand Tour call-up never comes, how do we immerse ourselves in these three, annual, twenty-one-day epics?

A bike race in person is undoubtedly a thing to be experienced. One hundred and eighty cyclists arcing and swirling like starlings on display. The arrow head of lead-out men pulling things along. The air crackling as a flock of fast-moving bikes hits you as a wind in the hair and a thud in the chest. It's a noise, and a punch-in-the-guts blur, and then it's gone.

At ease.

Nothing to see here.

Get on with your day.

But if you want to *watch* a bike race rather than *feel* it you need a TV, a clear diary, and an understanding family.

Supplement this coverage with websites, podcasts, and the occasional piece written by a Fotheringham and published in a broadsheet newspaper and you've got the whole shebang not so much covered as pinned down, dissected, and examined like an unfortunate frog at the desk of a biology student.

Be advised: what follows are not time gaps, power outputs, tactical debriefs, or cold hard facts. This book will take you through the Grand Tours of 2018, and it's all true. But it's *my* truth.

Just a pro cycling fan, sitting in front of a TV, trying to unravel what the heck Carlton Kirby[1] is talking about now.

---

[1]*Carlton Kirby, Eurosport commentator extraordinaire, considers any sentence not containing a play on words as grammatically incorrect. And what bike race wouldn't be enlivened by such gems as: "He's huffing and puffing now, blowing his invisible tuba...you could almost cut the silence with a banana!"*

Giro d'Italia

The Giro d'Italia, the first Grand Tour of the year, comes in May. Romantic, dramatic, and vaguely obscure, it's the choice of the connoisseur. It provokes a misty-eyed reverence that other Grand Tours lack. More extreme and less predictable that the Tour de France, more energetic than the Vuelta Espana. Full of hungry riders with fresh legs.

Each day, as the flag drops, a barely known Italian, in fluorescent kit and under sponsor's orders, will attack the race at full pelt. A guerrilla raid against the control-freakery of the big teams. From there, any semblance of control is a negotiation.

And geographically, of course, Italy has it all; mountains, coastlines, sweeping highways and winding villages. Throw in the unpredictable meteorology of May and it delivers in spades. Baking sun one moment, torrential rain the next, and sometimes, as if summoned for TV, vertiginous mountain roads sliced between six-foot snowdrifts.

Which, for a pro cyclist, is a *great* look.

The Giro is cool and knows it; the edgy indie move to the summer crowd-pleaser of the Tour de France. Rising soon-to-be superstars share the screen with fading legends in need of a career boost. Think Pulp Fiction, with less violence and more pasta.

Win the Tour de France and you're made for life - a Hollywood A-lister -but win the Giro and you get to be Uma Thurman; mysterious, credible, and cool. Not a bike rider but an icon. An artist.

The 2018 edition, the one-hundred-and-first Giro d'Italia, covered three-thousand-five-hundred kilometres over three weeks and twenty-one stages. It began in Jerusalem, took in a flying three-day tour of Sicily, before wending its way north.

Impossibly beautiful villages were traversed, historical monuments were lingered over, and the mountains of the Alps and Dolomites did their thing. Fans cheered, cyclists suffered, and the whole parade rolled into Rome to crown a winner.

It was, as it always is, *bello e brutale.*

Beautiful, *and* brutal.

stages 1-3: JERUSALEM

stage 1

I know it to be true. I can see it with my own eyes, and those on the ground seem happy to vouch for it, so I'm giving it the benefit of the doubt. But still: The Giro d'Italia, racing around the streets of Jerusalem? It's incongruous. It's implausible. It's a leap of faith.

It's taking some effort to quieten that part of my brain that suspects something fishy. The part that's nudging me and asking questions like: "Would it really be that difficult to stage a bike race on a film set on the outskirts of Turin?" and "are we sure the cut-away camera shots of Israel aren't stock footage?"

Just as I'm joining the dots and disappearing down the rabbit hole of conspiracy comes breaking news. Chris Froome has fallen off his bike, innocuously, pre-race, on a practice run. The kind of blunder that used to be his forte. Sliding across the asphalt like a speed-skater losing it on a bend.

Froome is the star of a new addition to his blooper reel and we all tut, and nod, seeing fresh evidence of his ongoing decline. Froome fell off practicing and (reigning Giro champion) Tom Dumoulin didn't. Also, Dumoulin is handsome, a stylist, so we're only too happy to install him as pre-race favourite.

Stage one was a prologue; a short, well directed jab of a time-trail designed to get the blood flowing and create an early leader board.

Out on the roads (of Jerusalem, allegedly) handsome Tom was quick, and smooth, and arrowed his way around the twists and turns. He won the stage and now wears the Pink Jersey of race leader.

Froome, on the other hand, was tentative. Nervous. Was the crash playing on his mind? Was the raw skin on his hip bones creating aerodynamic drag? Shall we roll out the era-ending retrospectives now or wait a few more days? These are the levels of deep-dive analysis the Team Sky leader's every action provokes.

Nerves, of course, are to be expected on the opening stage of a Grand Tour. I myself – seasoned armchair veteran of dozens of bike races –felt butterflies the moment I learned that Eurosport had paired Carlton Kirby with Sean Kelly[2] in the commentary box.

My heart thumped, and sweat began to bead up on my forehead. Kirby, and Kelly, in Israel, given free rein to ramble? Surely at some point the politics of the region would crop up. The idea that our

---

[2]*Sean Kelly, of course, being the uber pro cycling hardman of the 1980's; a man so blunt he can describe the delicate colours of a passing lavender field and make it sound like a threat.*

favourite double-act could avoid a diplomatic faux-pas for three hours seemed impossible.

How long before Kirby offers his own thoughts on the viability of a two-state solution, I wondered, *and just how badly might Kelly mangle pronunciation of Benjamin Netanyahu?*

I was on the edge of my seat.

I needn't have worried. With the usual random mid-race fixations to deal with – "thick legged time-triallists", Simon Yates' middle name (Phillip, for the record), and the ongoing challenge of making a man in tight clothes riding fast in a straight-line sound interesting – politics never got a look in. Not a sniff of regional tension.

As I sat down for the evening highlights on TV, I couldn't help noticing I *wasn't* surrounded by the smoking ashes of a post-apocalyptic world. Always a good sign. The day had gone off without incident.

For other Giro contenders like Fabio Aru, Miguel Angel Lopez, and Michael Woods, it was not so stress free. Losing a minute each, give or take, their respective challenges, after just ten kilometres, reduced to rubble.

On a flat stage in a Grand Tour the breakaway – that group of riders who escape the pack to lead the race – is crucial. Not because a member of that group will win, but for a variety of other reasons.

Pro cyclists are essentially rolling billboards. Their jerseys, shorts, shoes, shades, bikes, and beards are designed to promote brands and sell products. The best way to do this is to win bike races. The *second-best* way to do this is get yourself all over the TV. And the best way to do *that*, for most cyclists, is to get in the break on a Grand Tour.

Whatever disparate group pedal clear of the main field will play the starring role in your viewing pleasure for the day.

A typical breakaway will include a risk-taking chancer who's crafted a career out of visibly losing bike races; a veteran, with a back story, who you recognize; and some young pup from a wild-card team with a point to prove and the pedalling style of a baby gazelle.

For stage two, playing the role of recognisable veteran, was the rider with the most functionally efficient name of them all. No messing about. Two syllables.

You spot it, rattle it off, and get on with your day: Lars Bak. If you consider that early in the stage Guy Niv also attempted to animate the race it's clear that the riders were doing all they could today to get to the point; keeping the race rolling along and the surnames to a minimum.

An inconsequential detail, perhaps, but today, between Haifa and Tel Aviv, almost *every* detail was inconsequential.

The riders were going through the motions, wide-eyed and confused at the sight of Israel rushing past in their peripheral vision. Only Guillaume Boivin – of the Israel Cycling Academy, on home roads - managed to put up a fight, with a sterling yet so obviously doomed effort that the word doomed doesn't quite do it justice. I can only think to adopt the classic pro cyclist vernacular of prefixing any noun with *super-* for emphasis.

He attacked alone after the final climb of the day while the peloton, like an apathetic cat refusing to engage with a bedraggled ball of wool, left him hanging. When they eventually perked up for a sprint finish, he was super-doomed.

Apart from that, against the concrete backdrop of the Israeli motorway network passed kilometre, after kilometre, after kilometre, of not very much. Only Team BMC bothered to breathe life into proceedings, propelling Rohan Dennis[3] into the leader's pink jersey with the time bonus at the second intermediate sprint.

And the fact that I'm about to talk you through the nuances of that second intermediate sprint, frankly, says it all.

---

[3]*We can't ignore the fact that Sean Kelly, on the Eurosport coverage, continues to persist with "Ronan" Dennis rather than the infinitely more correct "Ro-han". I can only assume he thinks the BMC man is a fellow Irishman and he's trolling Dennis's parents*

Because intermediate sprints, you see, don't normally have nuance, and if they do, they are of the parochial mid-race variety. They're certainly not for public consumption. Contenders for the points jersey sprint half-heartedly, powder is kept dry, and face is saved.

But Rohan Dennis and his team had a plan. They'd identified the time trial on stage *one* as a chance to take the race lead but Tom Dumoulin, as we know, had begged to differ. Today's mid-stage time bonus was their chance to snatch the Pink Jersey[4] from the Dutchman. It was polite, well mannered, revenge.

Dennis laid the groundwork early, reportedly flitting around the peloton in negotiation to figure out who might challenge them. What this negotiation involved is unclear. The image of the Aussie, with a roll of fifties, slipping them one by one up the Lycra thigh grippers of selected riders, is one entirely of my own making.

We can't say for sure whether this actually happened. For the sake of our incident hungry imaginations and to liven up a dull day, let's assume it did.

Once the cash was safely tucked away Tom Dumoulin appeared ambivalent about holding such an early race lead. Elia Viviani, the Italian sprinter and man most likely to win a sprint finish, was happy

---

[4]*Were I a corporate, Giro man, I would now be referring to the Fight for Pink (or, more accurately, the #fightforpink). Thankfully, for you, I won't. There are many jokes I could make about this marketing mis-step, none of which I consider tasteful enough for publication.*

for BMC to take the initiative. So off BMC went, bossing the intermediate sprint and snaffling precious seconds for their man.

Job done.

Finally, as the road entered Tel Aviv, the peloton woke up to the dangling carrot of a Grand Tour stage win and quickened towards a heavily populated sprint on a wide city street.

The voice of Eurosport's Rob Hatch rose one octave, then another, as Viviani surfed the wheels, biding his time. Thinking clearly at seventy kilometres per hour (Viviani, not Hatch) the Italian slithered along the barriers and hit the front, to win in formidably uncomplicated fashion by what seemed like a hundred metres.

TV replays confirmed a more plausible three bike lengths.

Either way, it was a few extra Euros in the bank, some champagne on the podium, and perhaps the greatest prize of all for an Italian sprinter in the Giro d'Italia: when legendary king-of-the-Giro Mario Cipollini starts bad mouthing the quality of sprinting in the race (he always, at some point, announces to anyone within earshot that he could still beat them all now, today, in this race, at the age of fifty-one) Viviani gets to answer back.

To *actually* silence the *actual* Mario Cipollini is not realistic, but with a sprint win in the bag Viviani can at least now rise above it. As for the Greatest Race in The Most Beautiful Place™ we can only hope today was a blip.

Yesterday's winner, Elia Viviani, suffers from an affliction common among cyclists. Estimates suggest as many as 99.94% of all professionals are affected. In most cases it's diagnosed at birth, and although the condition can be managed it is, as things stand, untreatable.

An otherwise un-humanly fit and healthy man, Viviani has a chronic and debilitating case of *not* being Mark Cavendish, Marcel Kittel or Andre Greipel.

Symptoms include a lack of Grand Tour stage wins (a solitary Giro stage in 2015), and persistent disrespect from cycling fans. Viviani, who's won a ton of medals on the track (including Olympic Gold, no less, in 2016), can only wonder just how glittering his career might have been had he not been struck down. It's a cruel blow.

But in life, success and failure are often dictated by the company we keep. In the same way that alcoholics often surround themselves with other alcoholics (ideally in some kind of support group, rather than a pub), in this year's Giro d'Italia he is sharing the road with a peloton packed with fellow sufferers.

This levels the playing field somewhat, and on a level playing field he's the class act.

Although many of us nodded off during that functional stage two schlepp along the main roads into Tel Aviv, I'm reliably reminded by a crack team of insomniacs within my friendship group that Viviani took the win in style. I'm yet to hear word from Mario Cipollini – the retired forty-two[5] time Giro stage winner - on the impressiveness (or otherwise) of this.

I picture him in the gym of his five-star hotel, raging against his fifty-one years of age, pumping iron in front of a fifty-inch screen showing re-runs of his greatest triumphs from the 1990's.

He *knows* he could still beat Viviani.

But what more can Viviani do?

Today, on stage three, he shrugged off his challengers to win again. The patience he showed as the sprint wound up – at one point he appeared to whip a copy of Cycling Weekly out of his jersey pocket for a bit of light distraction – was that of a man completely at ease with his status as the fastest man in the race.

When you know you're the strongest you let others make their move first. Although he was bumped by Sacha Modolo and barged by Sam Bennet (narrowly avoiding an untidy rendezvous with the safety barriers) he used his shoulders, found another gear, and won the sprint finish with room to spare.

In 2017 I saw Viviani in the flesh at the Six Days of Ghent track event. He was confident and charismatic, and carried the aura of a

---

[5]*Yes, forty-two stage wins is a lot. An awful lot. One might even describe it as "eyebrow-raising." The hows and whys of this would fill a book on their own, written by someone with good lawyers. Let's just agree that they involved doping allegations, animal print skinsuits, a Julius Caesar complex, and a professed alternative career as a porn star.*

world-class cyclist around the curves of the Kuipke stadium. He worked the crowd, played the fool, and dished out several spells of devastating power.

If you looked away from the track for a moment and then looked back again your eyes were drawn immediately to Viviani, standing out - somehow smoother and stronger - before the mass of twenty-odd other cyclists came back in to focus.

It's how I imagine Taylor Swift looks in a party full of C-list celebs; a glittering sphere with shaved legs and a gravitational pull. Just immediately better.

Of course, if Peter Sagan had rolled onto the track and joined the fun (or Beyoncé had sashayed into the party shaking her booty), the stakes are raised.

The dynamic changes.

Safe to say, though, that close up Viviani reminds a rank amateur like me, with a beer in one hand and a hot-dog in the other, just how many rungs up the ladder he really is. For fellow sufferers of not being Cavendish, Kittel or Greipel, the man is an inspiration.

Today, ultimately, there was really no way to dress up the fact that stage three was similar to stage two but with extra sand and additional camels; it was a bit longer, the start and finish towns were more obscure, but it was a formulaic affair against a backdrop of desert gloom.

A guest appearance from Swift, Beyoncé, or Sagan, could only have improved matters.

And as this three-stage "Big Start" in Israel ends, and the race rolls on to Italian soil for stage four, we give our verdict.

In principal the Grand-Tour-start-in-another-country-honestly-we're-not-doing-this-for-the-money schtick is not a problem. I get it. It's capitalism.

But on the Israel experiment, from the perspective of someone who knows a good bike race when he sees one, I have my own three-word summary: roll on Sicily.

stage 4

Yesterday was a day off at the Giro d'Italia, as the riders were transported from Asia to Europe, Israel to Italy. Officially a rest day. And pro cycling folklore has it that strange things happen on a rest day.

The riders all go for a bike ride, for starters. Keeping the legs supple and the system ticking over. Ensuring the body doesn't tip too far into recovery mode. The accumulated, mythical rules of the sport[6] and the number-crunched sports science is in agreement on the wisdom of this.

But more sinister forces are also at work. The most damaging of which can cause a cyclist's form to evaporate.

---

[6] *Over the years, many examples of the right way to go about being a pro cyclist have found their way into folklore. You can eat the crust of a baguette, for example, but never the interior – the inside bit is light and fluffy, see, making your leg muscles light and fluffy. Or something. It was a simpler time.*

A thousand variables - the weather, the hotel room, the food, the sleep, the position of the moon in relation to Eddy Merckx's home town – can come together and turn *good legs* into bad. The gods of cycling have spoken; riding well or riding badly is less to do with training and sacrifice and more to do with the whim of *the legs*. From contender to bunch-filler in twenty-four hours and no amount of sports nutrition can stop it.

There is, perhaps, just *one* other factor to consider. It relates to the amount of down-time the riders have and the corresponding quantity of Nutella they eat. Alone. In a hotel room. From a jar. With a spoon. Leaving the cleaners to wonder about the apparent "dirty protest" on the bed sheets.

Because pro cyclists, as we know, are addicted to Nutella. As a delivery system to inject some dirty carbohydrate into a depleted cyclist's system there is probably an optimum amount of Nutella. And then a tipping point beyond which all manner of "bad legs" lie. I would wager that if someone likes to eat Nutella from a jar with a spoon their relationship with moderation is tenuous, at best.

To make matters worse the three days *prior* to the first rest-day of this Giro d'Italia were spent heaving in great lungs full of Israeli desert sand, and the rest-day itself involved a dawn call and a three-and-a-half-hour flight back to Italy.

A nice, relaxing, flat stage was just what the doctor ordered.

What was delivered was a couple of hundred kilometres of Sicily; dog-eat-dog, on ragged roads, approximately three kilometres of which were flat.

The peloton rattled along, chasing breaks and counter-breaks, and tired riders crumbled from the back of the race like a breadcrumb trail marking the way home.

With seven kilometres to go, on the approach to the ancient and historic finish town of Caltagirone, came a pinch point. The road narrowed without warning and a slow-motion pile up of riders ended the day of anyone the wrong side. All that Nutella, perhaps, leaving a once skinny peloton too wide for the road?

And then, in the final run-in, came a shiny, slippery, hairpin bend. Designed in, and perhaps polished rigorously the night before, for the purposes of jeopardy and tension?

By now the riders were full-gas through narrow streets – the kind that end up on postcards and in holiday brochures. Houses high on either side. Balconies peering in. Crowd noise echoed and amplified. Fans baying.

And then, on the steep ramp to the finish, came the composure of Tim Wellens[7]. Diligently delivered into position by a succession of

---

[7]*Tim Wellens is a stylist: long of leg, flat of back, and a deliverer of graceful brutality on a bike. If you like your cyclists to be all-conquering super-humans then Chris Froome or Peter Sagan are probably the guys for you. Wellens represents something different: a fluid style and a quiet stillness. If you ever need to quote an example of a "stylish Belgian" (it's a niche area, I know), then Wellens is your man*

teammates he was away, and off the front, on the short and punchy climb to the finish – as terrain goes, it's meat and drink to a Belgian cyclist.

He had three rivals for company.

Wellens peered, and then peered again, over his shoulder. He could see the finish line, we could see the finish line, but only *he* knew there was another move to make. He waited, the riders jockeyed for position, then BANG! One more attack and *the legs* gave their blessing; all in, eyeballs out, for the win.

More excitement in ten kilometres than in three stages worth of Israel, and the Giro d'Italia is underway.

stage 5

It's stage five and we're still in honeymoon mode. That magical early promise, all adorable secrets and quirky habits, hangs in the air. Routine is not yet established. The bride, of course, is early race leader Rohan Dennis. You, dear reader, are the groom. Or vice-versa. Or maybe it's a civil partnership? You get the idea – for the sake of a clunky analogy just go with me on this.

Tom Dumoulin had flirted with pink on stage one – an ill-advised fumble with an old flame – before Dennis started buying drinks and making small-talk. And now, on the roads of Sicily, he's busily consummating the relationship in front of a world-wide TV audience.

Bold.

Friends smile and make nice. The pretence is maintained but few, of course, think it will last. All predict the romance will unravel, perhaps with a spat in the full glare of a boozy dinner party, or maybe out on the road, on stage six, on the slopes of Mount Etna.

The main contenders will flex their muscles and Dennis will be digging out the pre-nup and on the phone to his lawyer. At some point the Pink Jersey, and the race lead, will move on, and the likes of Dumoulin, Froome, Yates, and co. will swoop in to pick up the pieces.

But before Etna, stage five gave us a second, less frantic day in Sicily.

A short stage with a relatively gentle opening, riders were spotted signing on late and sauntering around in the shade at the start, like freshly landed holiday makers, floppy limbed and carefree, eyeing up the talent around the pool.

Those in the know reported that Simon Yates, a man looking in particularly fine fettle thus far, was in the best mood anyone can ever remember; a coded message, if ever I heard one, that Yates is normally a right grumpy sod. Or that you should wander on down to your nearest bookmaker and place a small wager on him to win.

Or both, perhaps.

For most riders, with one eye on Mount Etna – literally, for much of the time, as it glowered from its high point on the Sicilian horizon – legs were being saved. At least until the traditional (can two consecutive occasions be a tradition?) uphill sprint finish in a Sicilian town, at Santa Ninfa.

Forty-odd sprinters-who-can-climb and climbers-who-can-sprint strung themselves out on the ramps of the finish – a slightly more nuanced affair than the power-fest we saw on stage four. Tim Wellens was fancied for a second win but Enrico Battaglin, the Italian, found prime position and picked his moment to sweep past Giovanni Visconti, another Italian, to take it.

Coming not-so-hot on the heels of his last Giro stage win four years ago.

Battaglin, you see, likes to race on home soil. Of those career wins that you might describe as *major* bike races he has three stage wins at the Giro. And that's that. He's a one-trick pony with a particularly impressive and geographically consistent trick.

You may be aware that Battaglin is a famous name in Italian cycling. *Giovanni* Battaglin won both the Giro d'Italia and the Vuelta Espana in 1981, and the Polka Dot Jersey at the Tour de France in 1979. Impressive. That's officially legend territory. His name lives on as the founder of the bike manufacturers that bear his name.

He's from the town of Marostica, in the region of Veneto, northern Italy, as is today's winner Enrico. And yet Enrico Battaglin claims to be no relation, and stakes no claim as the heir to the Battaglin family business.

No-one believes him, of course.

We cycling fans love a sentimental tear-in-the-eye narrative and what's better than a father-son Giro stage winning double act with added side-line in high-end bike manufacture? *Nothing's* better, that's what.

So, whatever anyone else may claim, and just to clarify: the winner of stage five was Enrico Battaglin, son of Giovanni and heir apparent to the Battaglin bicycle empire.

And what of those potential partners for pink?

Chris Froome looks eminently human[8], drifting backwards through the field towards the finish and losing precious seconds. The "obituaries" have been drafted if not yet published.

Miguel Angel "Superman" Lopez took a dive into a grass verge and emerged dishevelled– perhaps his cape got tangled in the workings of his bike?

Pinot is Pinot, so who knows?

Yates looks perky and strong.

And defending champ Dumoulin remains calm and composed, keeping his head down and biding his time.

---

[8]*Here in the UK Chris Froome is not universally popular. There are many reasons for this. One thing is for sure, though: the more human he becomes, the more popular he'll be. In a world where "human" means unsuccessful and "popular" means he'll have a lesser volume of bodily fluids thrown at him.*

Sicily itself peaks tomorrow with the ascent of Mount Etna. A big, and quite possibly final, day as race leader for Rohan Dennis.

stage 6

"You can feel as good as you like but it isn't worth a pinch of shit if the other guys are feeling better."

So said George Bennett, today; cyclist, New Zealander, and official antidote to the media-trained pronouncements of professional sport.

On the stage six struggle up this famous volcano only three guys, as it happened, felt better than Bennett. For two of those - Esteban Chaves and his Mitchelton-Scott teammate Simon Yates[9] - the summit finish on Mount Etna was the very definition of a perfect day.

The Colombian was away in the breakaway all stage, and when he made his final attack on the climb of the volcano he looked uncatchable – until Yates (officially, now, *the* form man in the race) rolled up alongside and shepherded his pal home for the win.

Yates could've ridden past Chaves and won the race himself but didn't. It was a touching moment between teammates and a display

---

[9]*Simon Yates is from Bury, Lancashire, in the north of England. To hear him speak you'd do well to identify that fact. He has taken over from Irish veteran Nico Roche in having the least geographically identifiable accent in the pro peloton. So mixed and mangled is it by years of team buses and hotel rooms it straddles at least three continents and a dozen time zones.*

of Aussie mateship. "A classy gesture" in the words of team boss and professional Aussie Matt White.

And I know what you're thinking. You're thinking that Yates is a Brit, and Chaves is Colombian, and what's that got to do with Aussie mateship?

The fact is that the Mitchelton-Scott team, all sunshine smiles and positive vibes, couldn't be *more* Aussie if they replaced the mid stage feed-zone with a barbie and tied dangling corks to their helmets. Either way, whether due to mateship or simple contractual commitment, they took a one-two on the stage and now fill two of the top three places in the overall General Classification. Yates now holds the race lead. Also, the volcano didn't erupt. It's no wonder they were beaming from ear-to-ear. High-fives all-round.

Back in 2002, geography fans, Etna *did* erupt, creating a huge column of smoke and ash visible from space. Co-incidentally, first reports of Chaves' win today filtered through via the International Space Station from a pair of Cosmonauts who happened to be peering out of their porthole window at that very moment.

Along with plumes of volcanic ash, the Great Wall of China, and Mario Cipollini's ego, the vast smile of Esteban Chaves is one of those man-made structures clearly visible from beyond our earthly atmosphere.

Though I have to question the lengths some people will go to for a good view of a bike race; the years of astronaut training, the gruelling selection process, and some serious forward planning. It seems the Esteban Chaves fan club has some pretty dedicated members.

The truly significant moment of the stage (and potentially the Giro as a whole) came some kilometres *prior* to the finishing line. Until Yates made his move to join his buddy up the road, he was nestled quietly in the small bunch of contenders seemingly set to roll to the finish. And then he stood on his pedals, rolled ahead along the right side of the road, and looked back at his rivals for a slightly uncomfortable amount of time.

Via the medium of body language, he said: "Ok, so I'm just going to go ahead and attack now, would any of you chaps care to join me?"

Awkward.

Eye contact was avoided. Riders peered intently at the road, their feet, their front wheels; anything, in fact, that wasn't Simon Yates. Their collective response, also via the medium of body language, was: "No we're fine thanks Simon. Really appreciate you asking though. So, erm...see you at the top?"

And Yates was off. No-one felt able to follow. As statements of intent go that one was writ large in marker pen on a giant placard and waved in front of the peloton by a man dressed as a comedy gorilla. A metaphorical comedy gorilla.

It was a bold statement, is what I'm saying, and Yates is looking good.

stages 7-10: PUTTING THE BOOT IN

stage 7

Stage seven gave fans, teams, and journalists the first real chance of the 2018 Giro to get cross about Team Sky. *Now it feels like a Grand Tour.*

After the exertions of Mount Etna on stage six the riders faced a tricky evening transfer across to the Italian mainland for dinner, a rub-down, and the commencement of the nightly inter-team Sudoku competition (or whatever mischief fit and healthy young sportsmen get up to of an evening these days).

Boats were the agreed method of transport. Predictably, logistically, minor chaos ensued. Teams reached hotels late. Vast quantities of pasta were overcooked.

But Team Sky, as you might expect, had a plan. Dave Brailsford produced a stuffed money clip from his jeans pocket, waved it at the nearest helicopter pilot, and had his precious cargo loaded on board and whisked across the Strait of Messina.

Social media cried foul. 'A team with a big budget has a bit of an advantage' was the gist of the criticism (which rather ignores all the other advantages a team with a big budget has).

They also, presumably, got a head start with the Sudoku. Those bastards.

One person who *didn't* quite make the helicopter crossing was Chris Froome, delayed, apparently, by an inability to pee right up to the line on the glass beaker in the post-stage anti-doping portacabin. Another one of those occasions where we, the watching public, find ourselves dwelling on both the quality and quantity of urine produced by a fellow human being. It's the slightly humiliating yin to the yang of sporting glory.

Anyway.

Stage seven.

It's fair to say the main contenders saw it as a chance to take things easy and recharge the batteries by riding a mere one-hundred-and-fifty-nine kilometres. In lieu of anything particularly interesting to report I thought I would share a mid-afternoon entry from the live text commentary on the Cycling News website. It acts as a kind of summary of the day:

"15:36:03 CEST. 78km remaining from 159km. The riders are enjoying lunch on the road, eating rice cakes and small sandwiches. We can see Ballerini drinking a small soda."

I trust this paints a picture?

Tranquil, is a word that springs to mind.

I presume you're familiar with the "boot" of Italy? Today's stage began in Pizzo, a town on the metatarsal, before wending its way suggestively up the ankle, and finishing at the base of the tibia – the shin, in fact – in a town called Praia a Mare. The route presented a wide highway running along the Mediterranean coast.

This was our scenery for the day. Perfectly pleasant. Very little in the way of hills or other obstacles.

I, of course, put my mortgage on Elia Viviani to win a standard sprint finish, because why wouldn't I? He's Italian, and therefore motivated, he's the class sprinter in this race, and his team drive a pretty formidable lead-out train, having propelled him to win the two sprint stages thus far.

I've found a (metaphorical) baby and I'm stealing its (theoretical) candy whether you like it or not.

I didn't tell my wife about this bit of minor larceny - I didn't need to. She has absolute faith in my pro cycling knowledge.

The inevitable sprint finish arrived, and Bora-Hansgrohe's Irish fast-man Sam Bennett timed his effort to perfection to outflank both

Viviani and his compatriot Niccolò Bonifazio and take the win. His first in a Grand Tour. A stunning finish from Bennett, upsetting Viviani's ruthlessly efficient applecart and, unfortunately, rendering me homeless.

Which is a setback.

I'm happy for Bennett, really I am. And the mortgage company agreed they had fully expected Viviani to win too, which makes me feel a little better, if no more secure in my housing situation. My wife is being cagey about whether she too had pinned her hopes on the Italian, but then her mind is on other things.

She's out in the garden at the moment burning my cycling kit.

My misjudgement was based on more than just an appreciation of, and therefore a bias towards, the silky sprinting skills of Viviani. The fact is Sam Bennett was never on my radar.

It's a peculiarity of pro cycling that no matter how much of your life you spend sitting in front of the TV, listening to Sean Kelly describe the construction method of a tiny cyclist's sandwich[10] as they freewheel through the feed zone, certain riders will always pass you by.

---

[10] *I forget the race – possibly one of those long, hot, lethargic days in the Vuelta Espana. I was stretched out on the settee aimlessly watching the riders gather their lunch bags when it dawned on me. Sean Kelly is describing a sandwich: "what they'll have is a small bread roll, with maybe a little butter or mayonnaise just to moisten it, and it could be filled with ham, or cheese, or even something sweet like jam...". I am literally spending my afternoon listening to an ageing Irish man describe a sandwich.*

One-hundred-and-seventy-odd riders began the Giro back in Jerusalem and it's entirely possible that with a gun to my head and my family held to ransom I could recognise the names of only sixty percent of them. Even without this menacing scenario I'd probably manage sixty-five percent at best.

I'm not sure under what circumstances I might find myself forced to name cyclists at gunpoint, but who knows – it's a mad old world.

I think this mental dead spot was related to the generic simplicity of the name: Sam Bennett. If that weren't enough, he is Peter Sagan's teammate, which makes him, simply, a rider in a Bora-Hansgrohe jersey who isn't Peter Sagan.

Except that now he's a Grand Tour stage winner who ruined my life, and he's suddenly *very much* on my radar.

stage 8

The climb to the summit finish at Montevergine di Mercogliano was a slow burner. A long climb, with a shallow gradient, and for much of it all was quiet.

Race leader Simon Yates and the other contenders rode tempo, and it seemed the breakaway might have their day. But as the summit approached the rain got heavier, the hairpins more numerous, and the theatrics of another mountainous Giro stage revealed themselves.

Under dark skies and on wet roads the riders were spot-lit in the glow of motorbike headlights, like a Shakespearian crowd scene on a West End stage.

The tension increased and the peloton became interested in time gaps and bonus seconds and diligently reeled back the breakaway. Nerves began to jangle and Chris Froome added another act to his personal comedy of errors: he fell off, riding uphill. The only rider to fall, he revealed another chink and yet more evidence that he's out of sorts.

Thereafter he was jittery, occasionally wobbling and bumping others, and making furious radio contact with someone, about something. All is not well. In fact all is decidedly odd.

Perhaps we are witnessing the mental toll being taken by the "Salbutamol situation?"

For that small handful of pro cycling fans who are still unversed (and, indeed, interested) in the difference between a positive doping test and an adverse analytical finding, allow me to elucidate.

Back at the Vuelta Espana of 2017 Chris Froome *did not* fail a doping test. No sir-ee. That did not happen. What *did* happen was that he returned an adverse analytical finding for a specified substance. Still with me? Need a double espresso?

He was treating his asthma, as per usual, with Salbutamol delivered by an inhaler.[11] Salbutamol isn't banned, so no problem there. But it is a "specified substance" which means the authorities like to keep an eye on it. Where levels in the urine are found to be raised above a tolerated concentration the rider has provided an "adverse analytical finding."

The lawyers love this. They set their meters rolling, whack up the hourly rate and put their feet up on their desk for several months. We, meanwhile, become so familiar, through media reports, of the composition of Chris Froome's urine, that if we close our eyes and *really* concentrate, we can almost taste it.

Froome continues to race, meanwhile, and Sir Dave Brailsford and the Team Sky image machine answer any questions by picking their words very, very carefully.

The effect on Chris Froome is that the media circus following him gets bigger in size and more pointed in question. He would have to be an actual robot not to feel a tad under pressure during this legal go-slow. Hence, perhaps, the lapses and the struggles in this race to date?

---

[11]*Fun fact: Team Sky boss Sir Dave Brailsford doesn't use the term inhaler – he calls it a "puffer". Something about such an obviously Alpha male using this sing-song childlike language tickles me. The cynic in me wonders if he is managing events. That the Team Sky media gurus have concluded the word "puffer" makes it sound less naughty than "inhaler" and therefore increases Froome's chances of avoiding sanction. Can you see what this f****n' sport has done to my mind!?*

On Montevergine, in contrast, Simon Yates was serene. Tom Dumoulin was working hard but in control. Thibaut Pinot sensed weakness and attacked in the final kilometres – sprightly, like a Border Collie in a field of unruly sheep. But by this time the Ecuadorian wonder-kid Richard Carapaz was away, and clear, and bound for his, indeed his country's, maiden Grand Tour win.

Impressive.

I imagine Alejandro Valverde (not racing here), Carapaz's teammate and leader - in spirit, if not always out on the road - of their Spanish Movistar team, was watching on with interest. And when I say "interest" I mean he was sitting in a leather swivel chair, in a volcano shaped lair, stroking a cat and making plans.

Valverde[12], you see, is not averse to a mind game or two, even when it involves his own teammates. He's the pantomime villain we love to hate due to his, ahem, *history*, and relationship with transparency. If I were Carapaz I'd watch my back. And my front. And I'd probably monitor any suspicious activity around my sides, too.

In the last knockings of today's stage Froome held the wheels, just, to avoid any time losses. But at the finish he looked rattled, ashen faced, and like a very lean, wet rabbit in those moto headlights. If you

---

[12]*Just to be clear, I've never met the man, and am basing this solely on the way he butchered Spanish teammate "Purito" Rodriguez's attempts to win the World Championship road race in 2013 in favour of his Portuguese Movistar teammate Rui Costa, and his just-so villainous stubble. Oh, and also that history, that I so euphemistically italicise.*

stuck a rash fiver on him to win the Giro there are currently no signs you'll be getting a return on that.

Analytically speaking, the findings are adverse.

stage 9

It's official. As of stage nine Simon Yates and his Mitchelton-Scott team are dominant. Yates himself took the win on the summit of Gran Sasso d'Italia today with beaming teammate Chaves in third. They occupy the top two places on the General Classification. They are controlling the pace of the race, protecting Yates when needed, and placing him at the sharp end when the moment is right.

Perhaps *most* impressively they've achieved the near impossible in reprogramming the very brain of pro cycling: more than fifty percent of fans have now, according to official data, finally stopped referring to them as Orica (former headline sponsor, since 2012). For Mitchelton-Scott this Giro has been a marketing exercise at the synaptic level.

Were Team Sky exercising this level of control on the road and in the mind – and let's be honest, they usually are – the lower reaches of the internet would be glowing red with disdain. The comment sections would be awash with negativity, accusation, conspiracy theory, and several feet of inane doping chat.

The Aussies are currently in the privileged position of *not* being Team Sky, both literally and metaphorically. Yes, they're dominant, but they're *different* dominant. Also, neither Yates nor Chaves have spinny-legs and waggly elbows and the fundamentally conservative world of pro cycling likes that they look like "proper" cyclists.

Were they to eventually win this Giro d'Italia and *then* go on to dominate much of the rest of the season, and *then* spend the off season topping up their ranks with the best cyclists money can buy, and *then* take a heck of a long time to explain some medical issues using language written by lawyers, it's quite possible they might also become the *metaphorical* Sky. But we're not at that point. They're a likeable Aussie team with a couple of potential Grand Tour winners and a whole billabong full of goodwill.

We can count ourselves lucky that today they delivered perhaps their greatest tactical move of the race so far from the safe distance of another *actual* continent: they had twin Yates brother Adam take to the start line at the Tour of *California*. Visible proof, in a preemptive strike against the keyboard warriors, that they haven't simply been switching the near-identical twins, stage by stage, day-on-day-off, on the Giro.

Had Adam *not* been racing in America this particular conspiracy theory would surely have reared its ugly, doppelganger of a head.

Discussion about style on the bike, eye-colour, and distinguishing features would've rumbled. Ill-informed debate about whether Adam could theoretically be providing Simon's post stage urine[13] for the testers would have ensued.

Perhaps a new rumour, surrounding a mysterious "third" Yates, a triplet, not racing in California and playing some undefined but no doubt nefarious role in Simon's current dominance may still surface. But as it stands my (admittedly timid) excursions into comment-world suggest we are not yet plumbing those depths.

But I digress.

Back at the Giro, on that climb up to the Gran Sasso, today's peloton were stretched collectively on a high-altitude rack. Twenty-odd kilometres of gradient took them gradually above the snow line to be met by the steepest slopes in the final kilometres. Pinot, Pozzovivo, Chaves and Carapaz – strong climbers all –gritted, grimaced, and duelled, while Yates gave it some more body language. Out of the saddle, expressionless, looking around at his rivals – is he even breathing?

He delivered his move in the final hundred metres and took the win. A smile appeared mid-effort, when victory was assured. A howl of joy as he crossed the line - phew...*aaannd* breathe.

Chris Froome, meanwhile, continued to struggle, losing a further minute-and-some and describing stage nine as a "tough, tough day."

---

[13]*We're not yet half-way through the Giro d'Italia and already "urine" looms large in any keyword search. Now you're thinking about the quality, consistency, and flow-rate of Adam Yates urine, aren't you? You pervert!*

Talk of "re-evaluating during tomorrow's rest day" was, like his regular drip-drip of lost time, very un-Froome-like.

Meanwhile, my extremely reliable sources (Eurosport) out in California delivered a confirmed sighting of brother Adam for the purposes of an alibi.

An absolute master-stroke.

stage 10

For stage ten the organisers, proud Italians all, pulled out all the stops; full culture, maximum history, and a side order of pasta. The local tourist board milking the situation for all they're worth.

The stage began in Penne; a beautiful and ancient town with a history going back to the mid-Neolithic period. Historic and picturesque, it's a lovely place to start a bike race.

Mid-Neolithic, you may be aware, is a heck of a long time ago. It predates all the other "eras" that you may be familiar with: the EPO era, the Indurain years, Bernard Hinault's eleven-year war (1975-1986). We're talking pre-Coppi, here. And to cap it off the town shares its name with a pasta: the tube-y one that you get in the supermarket.

You may now be bracing yourself for a series of cheap gags on this topic. It's true that I never normally shy away from hanging a whimsical piece of pro cycling analysis onto a flimsy joke, but I'm trying to be high-brow. If we were in a town called Strozzapreti things might be different – my Strozzapreti banter is world class. I always

42

say that if a writer can't riff on a style of pasta known as the "priest strangler" then they're in the wrong business.

Alas, there is no town called Strozzapreti. Whatever pasta the riders *do* favour, though, they'd have been wise to carb-load, with today being the longest stage of the race at a calorie consuming two-hundred-and-forty-four kilometres.

Wending out of the region of Abruzzo and into Umbria, up hill and down dale (or whatever the Italian translation is: *sucollina e vallegiù*, perhaps?), to finish in another achingly, painfully, unfeasibly beautiful and historic town: Gualdo Tadino.

Italy are now officially trolling Israel. In your FACE, Tel Aviv!

As for the racing? You remember when I put my mortgage on Elia Viviani the other day and I ended up homeless? Well, today I decided predictions were out of the window. This proved to be a wise decision.

The big news revolved around Esteban Chaves and the disappearance of that trademarked smile. He lost twenty-five minutes (!) on the leaders, struggling badly on the very early, very big climb of the day. There was lots of conjecture; pollen allergies? Bad legs?

Hmmm, maybe. I suspect a simple case of "hunger knock." Not enough "priest stranglers" for breakfast.

Whatever, Mitchelton-Scott are now a one-horse town, where the horse, of course, is Simon Yates, and the town is, erm, the team. But what a magnificent horse he is. All tiny, and pink.

This isn't working. My attempts at high-brow have led me down the blind alley of an ill-advised horse analogy. I should've stuck to the cheap pasta gags.

The stage winner, for anyone still reading, was Matej Mohoric of Bahrain Merida, he of the super-aero[14] position and the look of a baby-faced assassin. He broke away in the final kilometres and dealt with the challenge of Nico Denz of AG2R with disdain.

Mohoric, you just know, will be one of those riders who very quietly and without fanfare goes on to win a huge number of bike races – so clinical, and undramatic, is he. One day we'll turn around and he'll be thirty-two, with a dozen Grand Tour stage wins, a World Championship, a couple of Monuments, several Classics, and enough National Champion jerseys to sew a giant patchwork quilt for the whole Bahrain Merida team to sleep under.

And isn't that a lovely image?

Tomorrow the race begins in Assisi. Strap yourself in for a steady stream of (low-brow) St. Francis references.

---

[14]*In pro cycling, as we know, "super" is the prefix of choice. Races can be super-hard. Winners of those races are often super-happy. A rider's position on the bike can be super-aero. But beware - back in the 1990's and early 2000's cyclists were regularly super-well-prepared for big races, none more so than a certain Texan. That didn't end super-well.*

You've probably heard of Saint Francis of Assisi.

Great cyclist.

Legend has it he was an early adopter of power data to refine his training methods, and a committed proponent of reverse periodisation *way* before the Team Sky boffins cottoned on; low volume, high intensity training gave him more time to spread the word of Christ, you see.

He was often spotted around Assisi, being religious, kitted out in Rapha. I'm pretty sure their "Assisi" range hits the shops later this year. He is, after all, the original cyclist-named-after-their-home-town; the precursor to Sir Bradley of Kilburn and Pippo "the Peacock of Sandrigo" Pozzato.

Stage eleven ran from Assisi to the town of Osimo, in the Marche region, right on the bulging calf muscle of Italy. It was a short, punchy affair. As the road roller-coastered to a cobbled climb of a town centre finish all manner of pro cycling royalty threw their hats in the ring.

Once the day's break (featuring, among others, professional break-maker and archetypal Big Engine™ Alessandro DeMarchi and veteran time trialling all-rounder Luis Leon Sanchez) was reeled in, Tim Wellens and Zdenek Stybar picked up the familiar scent of a cobbled climb and launched themselves.

Big moves.

Potentially *winning* moves.

If I had to pick two guys to win a bike race for my life up a punchy cobbled climb then Wellens and Stybar would be somewhere near the top of that list. Though, if I'm honest, that list would also include a footnote requesting further information about how we'd got to this point.

Who is trying to kill me, and why? It seems like an odd way to dispense justice.

On the flip side, not many people get to have Ned Boulting and David Millar commentate on the tactical nuances of their demise. On balance, I suppose there are worse ways to go.

Thankfully, today, no-one died; though Stybar and Wellens ultimately failed with their potentially winning move. So far in this Giro d'Italia Simon Yates is very much the man in charge of that department. When it comes to winning moves he's the Alpha male and he's got the corner office, big mahogany desk, and personal coffee machine.

Through a corridor of noise he went, as the people of Osimo emptied their lungs for the leader of the Giro. He followed Wellens with the steely stock-still body position of a man who had at least three more gears to reach for were it necessary.

Tom Dumoulin chased, the best of the rest, with demented futility. Formolo, Pozzovivo, and Pinot followed first in dribs, and then drabs, and Yates did that little no-hands-wobble across the line that might yet become his trademark.

It was theatrical stuff in front of a roaring crowd. Reminiscent, in a way, of the finish of the Tuscan semi-classic Strade Bianchi which reaches a similar climax in Siena.

One minute the civility of café culture is happily bubbling away – old timers sip espresso and read the paper, couples make eyes at each other - before the noisy interruption of a clutch of cyclists tearing through the calm like a four-year-old birthday party spilling into a high-end restaurant.

The old timers tut, bemused. The couples barely notice. Simon Yates, the birthday boy, emerges through the sugary high of a Haribo-stuffed party bag.

A race leader on the attack is what every bike race needs. Yates is committed and relentless, a star being born before our very eyes.

I'm not too clear on the details of the Catholic canonisation process but I do know the Pope is a cycling fan. I realise Yates might have to die first, but when he does, may I suggest that the out-muscling of Stybar, Wellens, and Dumoulin on a steep cobbled climb might justify some official recognition.

Saint Simon of Osimo, perhaps?

stages 12-13: HEADING NORTH

stage 12

There's a sub-category of pro cyclist known as the sprinter-who-can-climb. Frenchman Arnaud Demare is one. Aussie Michael Matthews is another. And today, on stage twelve, Irishman Sam Bennett made absolutely sure that everyone knows he is one too.

These sprinters-who-can-climb[15] are specialists. Like giant turtles in the Galapagos of the pro peloton they have evolved to thrive in a very specific set of conditions: where the route profile suggests a sprint finish, but the flat route that gets the riders there is punctuated by hills.

---

[15]*They need a proper name, really, these sprinters-who-can-climb. This is such a mouthful. Usually the French have this kind of thing pretty well sorted out. A sprinteur, perhaps?*

The sprinters-who-can-climb are lean and lithe enough to hang on uphill and muscular enough to win the ensuing sprint. They can't win a hilly stage, and won't win a standard sprint; they need a bowl of mummy bear's porridge.

Just right.

The race organisers, working from paper, declared stage twelve to be flat; the route from Osimo to Imola disrupted by a single climb towards the finish. A climb of several kilometres in length and an average gradient of around four percent. Not a mountain. Not a berg. But a climb, nonetheless.

Sam Bennett fancied the sprint that would follow the descent – on the finishing straight of the motor racing circuit of Imola - and made sure to position himself well as the climb progressed. He was sprightly, and visible. In control among the first dozen riders. Until the last couple of uphill kilometres when suddenly he wasn't; he was otherwise engaged at the head of the field, nonchalant, looking around.

The race leader.

Like a 2009 Alberto Contador eyeing up the competition. Assessing his rivals for weakness. A show of strength. A sprinter-who-can-dance-on-the-pedals.

He soon tucked back in, wisely, perhaps, and strapped in for a wet descent on a twisting road to the racetrack and a gallop for the line.

By this point the torrential rain of the day had eroded any pretence of order and routine. The race was in pieces.

Bennett launched his sprint WAY too early, like a lead-out man who's forgotten his sprinter. He scorched past Ulissi and Betancur, the last of the day's attackers. His big rival, Viviani, was way back - several minutes, in fact - a sprinter-who-can-climb proving today that he couldn't. Conditions and circumstances put paid to him many miles ago.

And with that, Bennett had won. By default. Climber, lead-out man, sprinter, and two-time Giro stage winner. Surely, by now, a man in need of a nickname.

After a sprint win at Imola, the home track of the mighty Ferrari (aka the Prancing Horse), there can be only one contender.

Il Cavallino Rampante.

The Prancing Horse.

stage 13

The north is the cycling heartland of Italy – every great Italian cyclist either came from the north, or moved to the north.

Take the town of Isola della Scala in the Veneto region. A small place, home to around ten-thousand inhabitants, but the birthplace of two world-class Italian sprinters in the past fifty years. Not a bad strike rate. Especially since each of the two also happen to be multiple Grand Tour stage winners.

Fifteen between them, to be exact, at the time of writing.

Fourteen, four hours *prior* to the time of writing, because Elia Viviani was yet to win today's stage thirteen – a largely flat rumble from Ferrara to Nervesa della Battaglia. Also in Veneto, co-incidentally, only a hundred miles or so up the road from Isola della Scala.

Nicola Minali, our other Isola-born sprinter, has presumably already won the last of his Grand Tour Stages. If he wins any more at the age of forty-eight, I imagine the drug testers will be turning up pronto with a bottle and a thirst for urine.[16]

If you can imagine such a thing.

As if that weren't enough geography for one stage today's start town, Ferrara, is the home town of another man for whom the clarity of a cyclist's urine has been something of a preoccupation over the years: Michele Ferrari.

Yes, *that* Michele Ferrari.

Close personal friend of a certain Texan cyclist (among others). He of the lifetime ban for possession, trafficking, and administration of

---

[16]*As far as I'm aware, this is the first recorded use of the phrase "a thirst for urine" in an English-speaking publication without being preceded by the phrase "Bear Grylls." You're welcome.*

doping products. The bloke behind Lance's miraculous transformation from cancer survivor to greatest athlete of all time. With the science, the stopwatch, the EPO, the moving around in the shadows, the hushed tones, and the pre-occupation with power to weight ratio.

Starting a stage in Ferrara, one would think, is a bit like agreeing a sponsorship deal for a big race with Festina[17] whilst puffing away on one of Floyd's, of Leadville's[18], finest.

Whatever. We all move on, I guess.

Nicola Minali (remember him?) would've fancied a win today. Viviani, after being well beaten on stage twelve by Il Cavallino Rampante (I *knew* it would catch on) was clinical, and now has a tight grip on the Maglia Ciclamino. That's the sprinters jersey, my English-speaking friends. And we *did* have a classic sprinters finish.

In the final ten kilometres the pace got faster and the peloton got longer and straighter. Largely down to Tony Martin, who strung things out by sitting on the front and giving an archetypical Tony Martin impression. After which each team took turns to line up their lead-out and have it swallowed again.

All the while Viviani and his Quick Step crew sat tight. Watchfully.

---

[17]*Festina. A word which, to pro cycling fans, will always be followed by '...scandal.' Also, official timekeepers of every sports event ever.*

[18]*Floyd, as in Landis (one of Lance's old pals) and Leadville, as in Floyd's of Leadville; purveyors of medicinal cannabis products. Yes, really.*

Positioned beautifully down the left-hand side of the road, with a couple of hundred to go Viviani sprung from his saddle and threaded a very high-speed length of cotton through the eye of a particularly erratic needle. He went past everyone, is what I'm saying. Sam Bennett missed the moment. Viviani won by a country mile (about three bike lengths).

And alas, there was no post stage analysis from local boy Ferrari. By the finish I'd made my peace with using his home town as the start and was rather looking forward to hearing his verdict. Not his kind of stage, though. He was in the business of "preparing" Grand Tour winners, not bulky sprinters.

Also, I hear he keeps his head down these days, what with a lifetime ban to adhere to. Was he required, I wonder, to sit in a darkened room at the back of his house wearing noise-cancelling headphones and being periodically distracted by reruns of Lance's Oprah appearance?

Just to absolutely ensure he couldn't see, or hear, or even *think about* a professional bike race.

I'm pretty sure that's how these things work.

stages 14-15: ALPS AND DOLOMITES

stage 14

May 19th 2018 had long promised to be a special occasion for the British. Drama, pomp, ceremony, a sea of tiny plastic Union Jack flags and the breathless reverence of the commentary team. It was the big day. And it ended with the happy couple not married, not even in love with each other, but crossing the finishing line in first and second positions.

For Froome, something approaching redemption. For Yates, more fuel to the flames of a potential maiden Grand Tour win. British cycling royalty in all its finery. The Harry and Meghan[19] of the pro peloton.

---

[19]*19th May 2018, you see, was the day of the Royal Wedding, where Prince Harry and Meghan Markle got hitched. Happy Zoncolan day!*

The Mighty Zoncolan™, our cathedral for the day, had been looming for some time. Right there at the end of the alphabet, on the third Saturday of the race, and at the forefront of the rider's minds. Ten kilometres of pain and suffering.

With an average gradient of around twelve percent it's comparable only to the Angliru of Vuelta Espana fame. Between them the A-Z of how to hurt yourself on a bike.

There's something about that Z, and those brutal three syllables: ZON-CO-LAN. It even sounds hard. And yes, I did use the word "brutal", and I make no apologies for that.

We all know the word is overused to the point of meaningless in cycling; it's second only to "epic" in that respect. If you ever utilise "marginal gains" to tackle a "brutal" climb on an "epic day in the saddle" you really have nailed the Holy Trinity of cycling cliché.

But the Zoncolan is the brutal bar by which all epic-ness should be measured.

Point made?

It's quite hard.

Chris Froome, clearly, has had enough of the brutality being dished out in the form of words, sentences, and paragraphs in the cycling media, which have happily narrated his demise in this race. Pushing his buttons to the point, it seems, where he lashes out.

Froome was away and clear on the Zoncolan – juice in his legs and fire in his belly. A man on a mission. But come the final kilometre it looked, pedal stroke by pedal stroke, as if Yates would catch the embattled Sky man. He, all gritted teeth and spinny legs, while Yates, the stylist, ate up the Tarmac.

And them, on the final ramps, the winning moment came: for maybe the first time in fourteen days of bike racing Yates' face creased up in pain.

"OK," it said, "we're done..."

Froome is back in the game.

Last year's best man, Tom Dumoulin, on terrain that doesn't favour him (as if Monte Zoncolan favours *anyone*), played damage limitation to give away a mere thirty-one seconds to Yates. Pinot was limpet-like on Dumoulin's wheel. Lopez, Pozzovivo, and the rest, followed.

Each man crumpled as the line was crossed, wheeled away graciously by a kindly helper for who knows what: A drink? A sit down? A little cry?

All would be acceptable.

After all, when the big day comes, a few tears are always to be expected.

Back in the day, the accepted measure for whether a pro cyclist was capable of winning a Grand Tour was power to weight ratio.

Each year, legend has it, Lance Armstrong would ride up the Col de la Madone in the south of France at full pelt. His coach/doctor/handler, armed with a set of scales, a calculator, and a massive stopwatch around his neck in the style of Flavor Flav from Public Enemy, would crunch the numbers[20].

If Lance hit the magic mark he "knew" he would win the Tour that year.

Simple.

It was only *later* that we discovered that other numbers were also crucial: concentration of red blood cells; number of dollars finding their way to the bank account of Dr Ferrari; viewing figures for subsequent teary-eyed Oprah appearance.

On stage fifteen the peloton hit The Dolomites, each rider with a Zoncolan in their legs; the new, internationally recognised measure of Grand Tour winning potential for a pro cyclist. There is a magic number of Zoncolans that a pro cyclist must be able to ride at race

---

[20]*I may have invented the massive stopwatch but it's how I see Dr Michele Ferrari in my mind's eye. A fan of early, politically charged hip-hop.*

pace in the Giro d'Italia and then recover from in time for the following stage. That magic number is one[21].

Simon Yates met that threshold in style today, and demonstrated definitively that he can, indeed, win this Giro d'Italia.

He was spectacular.

Those of us who have watched Grand Tours in recent years have become used to cagey, tactical manoeuvrings between the big riders. Gain some time, then defend it. Conserve energy. Do what you have to and no more. Don't overstretch yourself. Not to downplay Chris Froome's wins in the Tour de France or the Vuelta Espana in 2017 but both were masterclasses in playing the percentages.

Yates, today, attacked off the front of the race with seventeen kilometres to go; a big, solo break, by the man in pink, with the aim of gaining as much time on Tom Dumoulin as possible before Tuesday's time trial.

You could argue that, as tactics go, it was his only option – Dumoulin is the far superior time-triallist and *will* gain time back - but that doesn't make it any less bold, brave, or indeed retro. He won the stage, finishing in the town of Sappada, handsomely.

---

[21]*Despite being a rank amateur I myself love to ride the big hard climbs that grace our TV screens each year. I relish the challenge. But I really don't want to ride the Zoncolan. Even slowly. It looks horrible.*

Froome, on the other hand, gave all the signs that his comeback on the Zoncolan yesterday was fleeting; he finished a minute and a half behind Yates. His Zoncolan rating at zero.

Others, too, in comparison to the majesty of Yates, struggled to deal with the effects of Zoncolan-legs. Italian Fabio Aru lost several weeks (give or take). As the TV cameras panned back repeatedly to pick him out, he gestured and gesticulated in the way that only an Italian can. Possibly ordering carbonara, more likely questioning the parentage of the TV director.

Either way he was suffering like a dog and did not appreciate that fact being broadcast to the watching world.

No such problems for smiling Colombian Esteban Chaves, a summit finish winner earlier in the race, lest we forget. He rolled home almost half an hour back, and out of range of even the most suffer-hungry TV cameras. Others – Pinot, Dumoulin, Pozzovivo, Lopez – minimised the damage at best.

All of which does rather put Yates's form into perspective.

At the finish he was clearly emotional. Voice cracking slightly, looking weary and fragile. Not, I suspect, a delayed response to the momentous union of Harry and Meghan the previous day, and more to do with a Zoncolan in the legs, a huge solo breakaway win, and the thought of a rest day tomorrow.

stages 16-17: THE CALM BEFORE THE...

To say today's time trial had been looming over this year's Giro would be an understatement. From the moment Simon Yates bridged up to teammate Esteban Chaves on stage six and gifted him a win at the summit of Etna, the subtitle of this race has been: "How much time can Yates gain before the time-trial?"

That was the day he'd looked like the boss of the race.

But Tom Dumoulin is the dominant time-trialler in the world right now. So, Yates climbs and gains time, Dumoulin grabs it all back in the TT, and we watch the remaining stages from the well-worn edges of our seats. Peroni in hand and big book o' cycling tactics across our laps.

Simple.

We say: "Yeah...so Dumoulin will gain probably two and a half minutes, minimum, on the TT, but then Yates will gain loads of time in the last three mountain stages..."

Blah-de-blah-de-blah. As if it's that simple. Because all this cycling can do funny things to the legs; it can make them tired, for example, producing muscles with the texture of jelly on the climbs and the consistency of pâté on the descents.

If I were Dumoulin I would retort: "You think it's that simple...YOU come and take two minutes and eleven off Simon Yates!" But I'm rash like that. Not diplomatic enough. Too emotional. I haven't had the media training. Just one more reason why I am not, currently, a Grand Tour contending pro cyclist.

And so, the time-trial arrived, right here on stage sixteen.

Never has a more crucial sporting event had so many people content to give the live feed a miss and catch up on the highlights. A few dozen cyclists riding quickly, one-by-one, on a flat road, has never been everyone's idea of entertainment.

The commentators will have no doubt been preparing late into the night, wracking brains and consulting the thesaurus for original descriptions of a skinny man riding quickly in an aero tuck.

The usual TV studio analysts, of course, are swapped out for slightly nerdy alternatives; experts in the art of the TT, with aerodynamic faces and a keen eye for a flat back. Cyclists for whom a non-descript A-road on a Sunday morning is their idea of Wembley stadium, and a cup of tea and a Victoria sponge in a parish hall has got the hospitality package covered.

They're purists. Man against clock. The race of truth.

I used to be a big fan of a TT. As a discipline I found it calming and meditative. The metronomic futility causing me to muse on the very nature of existence. Then the major bike manufacturers ruined it. With their rampant obsession for aero they began to create bikes whose ugliness increased exponentially in relation to their price tag.

Strange fairings began to appear, and seat-posts at funny angles; like a Picasso portrait, all the right bits were in there but the misalignment left a queasy feeling. I don't doubt they are quick, but look at them. There's surely a moment when the search for speed should give way to the time-honoured pillars of good taste?

Wilier, Italian bike makers par excellence, and creators of some of the most jaw-droppingly beautiful bikes imaginable, launched a bike so ugly recently that it caused a spike in my heart rate and a build-up of lactic acid in my calves. The very opposite of the reaction they were hoping for.

I now watch TT's with my hand in front of my face to obscure the bike, leaving me with only the bike-less wiggle of the rider on-board. It's really very inconvenient.

Nonetheless, I watched today's TT so you didn't have to, and this is what I saw: Rohan Dennis rode very, very fast, and won the stage. Tony Martin and Tom Dumoulin rode a bit slower, but still quite fast, to take second and third. Chris Froome rode well, which means tomorrow he'll ride horribly.

Thibaut Pinot sabotaged himself and lost over three minutes (clearly a selfless protest against the ugliness of the bikes – Vive le Pinot!), while Simon Yates lost a chunk of time but nothing like enough to lose the Pink Jersey.

He retains the race lead by nearly a minute and, although anything could still happen, the tension never came. Yates could have a bad day, or crash, or get sucked in and swallowed up by the sheer force of one of Eurosport commentator Carlton Kirby's swirling psychedelic analogies.

But, more likely, he could get all the way to Rome and win the thing.

Get the Peroni ready.

stage 17

It was not a simple, formulaic, sprint-friendly day, because this is the Giro d'Italia and they try and avoid those where possible. Frantic action teetering on the edge of chaos is the Giro's raison d'etre.

Stage seventeen didn't so much follow a script as follow several scrips, each one torn up and cast to the winds to be replaced by a new draft. A roomful of writers, back at Giro HQ, earning their money.

Attack followed attack, and break followed break, until the closing stages when everyone decided, after all, to settle in for a sprint. The Pink Jersey was safe and the sprinters were flexing their sun-baked muscles for a technical run through the town of Iseo and a gallop for the line.

"Too simple," declared race organiser Mauro Vegni, spinning round menacingly in a leather swivel chair and stroking an angry looking cat with a leather gloved hand: "...more drama!"

With barely two kilometres to race he reached for the button marked "monsoon" and the heavens opened. Performance enhancement: for the tension, the jeopardy, and the viewing figures.

Meteorological doping.

The lead-out men sped through town, an *actual* wake forming in their metaphorical one, Teams Bora Hansgrohe and Quick Step to the fore for their sprinters Sam Bennet and Elia Viviani.

Remember them? The stars of the show before the suffering and the drama of the mountains; still there, still pedalling, but visibly aged by the gruelling terrain. Skin tough and leathery. Faces lined like contours on an Alpine map. Thousand-yard stares.

All of that was for a day like this, and the chance of a sprint friendly(ish) stage win.

But the rain was coming in bucketfuls. Salmon were seen leaping against the flow of bikes and a cruel rip-tide put paid to local boy and potential stage winner Sacha Modolo's challenge. One down.

Van Poppel attacked early – *WAY* too early – all but aquaplaning through the small lake that sat where the finishing straight once was. Two down.

Viviani, on his man Sabatini's wheel, waited patiently, as he does. Sabatini peeled off, Van Poppel prepared to fade, and Viviani cranked his outboard motor and leapt clear. Bennett slotted in for second.

"Eccellente," purred Vegni, from his lair.

stages 18-20: BIG MOUNTAINS

stage 18

In the closing stages of a Grand Tour the race plays out on a knife edge. One moment Simon Yates is serene, in pink, as he has been for a couple of weeks. The next, Rob Hatch[22] on Eurosport is declaring crisis.

In the final two kilometres of stage eighteen Tom Dumoulin softened Yates up with one of his grinding diesel accelerations. Then Froome counter-attacked, Pozzovivo followed, and Dumoulin latched on to *his* wheel. Three prongs.

And in the two-metre gap that opened up between Dumoulin and Yates was the day's truth: "He's lost the wheel...oooohhhhh, and Yates is in crisis!"

---

[22]*Rob Hatch is a master of the commentator's art. Regardless of the actual words leaving his mouth he can communicate the complexity and nuance of any race situation through tone, volume, and cadence alone.*

Those two metres, in the context of the previous seventeen stages of dominant progress, were a chink in the armour. The other four best cyclists in the race spotted their chance and went hard. In the blink of an eye, from an impregnable position, Yates was into damage limitation. Just like that.

Finally, a bad day on the bike.

And this is what makes a Grand Tour a Grand Tour. The accumulated pummelling, mental and physical, tenderizes a rider like cheap steak. The muscle and cartilage dents, and bruises, and begins to lose integrity. Once one falls apart – mind or body – the other follows.

By the time they hit the summit finish line at Prato Nevoso Yates's overall race lead had halved; cut *by* 28 seconds, *to* 28 seconds over Dumoulin. *Probably* still the favourite to win.

I can almost hear the Aussie twang of Mitchelton Scott team boss Matt White[23] now:

"It's all good Yatesy...looking good in pink mate. You won't have seen Dumoulin 'cos he was twenty-eight seconds up the road but he looked knackered mate...cooked. He didn't even get half a minute on you...it was less than twenty-nine seconds. You're in pole position for tomorrow."

---

[23]*Matt White is to positive thinking what Thomas Edison is to the electric lightbulb. He pretty much invented it.*

But it's in the balance.

Stage nineteen, you feel – a massive mountain stage with a summit finish at Bardonecchia – will answer every question.

As for the winner of *today's* stage: German wunderkind Max Schachmann, from the day's breakaway, finished ten minutes clear of the main contenders for the win. Very happy for Herr Schachmann, first Grand Tour stage win, celebrations all round, but at what point can we admit we're officially bored of Belgian team Quick Step Floors winning bike races this season?

As my four-year-old son commented when I made this point to him: "I think they've won about infinity times, daddy..."

Make that infinity-and-one.

stage 19

If you're a masochist – and, if you take your cycling seriously, there's every chance you are – you might have enjoyed watching Simon Yates fall to pieces today on the slopes of the Colle della Finestre while Chris Froome took flight.

If, on the other hand, you're anything resembling a normal human being with a heart beating in your chest and a basic working knowledge of empathy, that heart will have broken just a bit.

It was trailed yesterday, as a mini-crisis, and today came the main feature. If you'd been hoping for happy ending to this finely crafted underdog storyline, look away now.

By the time the commentary team spotted the pink jersey number "118" hanging off the back of the race on the hairpins of the climb, Yates' Giro d'Italia was over. Swaying on the bike, form in tatters, and ninety kilometres of mountainous terrain to ride. Anyone who knows anything could see he was about to lose half-an-hour to his rivals.

A Grand Tour win gone, just like that.

He knew it, and we knew it.

Judging by the conspiratorial chat between Froome's Sky henchmen at the front, word had reached them too. Their punishing pace had done the damage. Pre-determined, you imagine, from that moment the day before when Rob Hatch had declared crisis. When they saw Yates morph from utterly impregnable into eminently fallible in just a turn or two of the pedals.

But that delivery of today's punishing pace was only act one. Act two came with eighty kilometres to go when Froome did the spinny-spinny thing and rode off the front. A bold move. From a frankly comical distance out.

Merckx-ian, dare I say?

And that was the last the others saw of him.

He won the stage by three-minutes-and-some and took the Pink Jersey from Yates (himself, more than half an hour behind). I'm going to write that again, just to see if it sounds the same. He won the stage by three-minutes-and-some and took the Pink Jersey from Yates.

O.M.G.[24]

Pro cyclists don't do this sort of thing. Not during Grand Tours, and certainly not when they're trying to *win* the whole three-week parade. Grand Tour winners ride percentages. They measure efforts and maximise gain. They have to ride tomorrow, you see, and then the day after that, and the day after that...

In a world without power meters and team radio, back when the bikes were steel and the kit was woollen, the likes of Merckx and Coppi would rattle off on these solo sorties from time to time. But the playing field has levelled since then. The gap between Campionissimo and also-ran is small.

To see Froome attack on the dirt and gravel of the Colle delle Finestre, dropping Yates, Dumoulin, and an entire peloton's worth of fellow cyclists, was impressive. To then continue watching as he clattered down the descent, dispatched the summit at Sestriere without blinking, and powered smoothly along the valley and the climb to finish at Bardonecchia, was something else.

---

[24]...*is what I would say were I twenty years younger.*

It was surprising, and confusing. It provoked a response on social media which was high-pitched and emotional.

Rational thought was by-passed in favour of the collective monkey brain.

Because cycling fans, with their craving for drama, excitement, and derring-do, can't quite bring themselves to trust it when it happens. Too much history. Several trunk-loads of baggage. But whatever you think of Chris Froome – a divisive figure in the cycling world – *that* was a big day on the bike.

Replete with doubts, slurs, and insinuation, it was Froome's masterpiece.

But what of Yates?

Is he the new (if infinitely more pronounceable) Steven Kruijswijk, who famously dominated the 2016 Giro, Yates-like, until he crashed into a snowdrift on stage nineteen and lost five minutes to Vincenzo Nibali? Snatching defeat from the jaws of victory.

Yates hasn't so much snatched defeat as taken it to a fancy restaurant, bought it dinner, and made eyes at it over the petit-fours.

He is now forty-minutes behind Froome. Forty minutes.

The Giro is gone.

Barring accident, Chris Froome will roll into Rome as the winner of the 2018 Giro d'Italia. The Giro has done what the Giro does.

Riders are scattered to the four winds; half the peloton rolled up the final climb of the race, to Cervinia, in the Gruppetto[25], forty-five minutes behind stage winner (and birthday boy) Mikel Nieve.

Limping. Straggling. The thought of a game of pass the parcel and big slice of cake wrapped in a napkin the only things keeping them going.

Dumoulin didn't so much throw the kitchen sink at Froome on the final climb as resemble someone carrying it, such was the arch of his back and the grimace on his face. But Froome was never really threatened in the end. Universal tiredness saw to that.

Thibaut Pinot, starting the day in third, cracked, and suffered, and strangled his way through the mountains. One of the day's forty-five-minute men along with stage nineteen casualty Simon Yates. To say

---

[25]*The gruppetto is the bunch of cyclists who form, off the back of the race, during mountain stages. Made up of sprinters and an assortment of exhausted, injured, or otherwise struggling riders, whose sole ambition for the day is to make the time cut.*

Pinot delved and rummaged around in Paul Sherwin's suitcase of pain[26] was putting it mildly; he was on the phone to the airline and arranging an extra luggage allowance in which to transport his suffering.

Pinot ended the day, and his race, in hospital. Exhausted, dehydrated, and plain unwell. Bonus points for effort, but Miguel Angel Lopez pinched his podium spot.

To cap it all off the internet is broken. Froome's miraculous comeback on stage nineteen, which created the winning position he defended today, saw the doping trolls swarm Twitter, evoking Lance and Landis[27], with cries of "not normal" (and worse).

History requires us to question every outstanding performance but were Froome French or Italian, a stylist on the bike, and not riding for Team Sky, would the response be quite so high pitched? Hard to say. The questioning is the only sensible course of action. The tone of the debate is ludicrous.

The Giro d'Italia of 2018 has been brutal, epic, and full of suffering – pick your own from pro cycling's drop-down menu of dramatic

---

[26]*Paul Sherwin was one half of the legendary Liggett-Sherwin commentary team double act; the definitive soundtrack to the sport for many fans. Sherwin, like all commentators, had his stock phrases to fall back on. A rider "delving into his suitcase of pain" was nonsensical and memorable in equal measure. Sherwin sadly passed away in 2018.*

[27]*Lance being Lance. As in Armstrong. He of the yellow wrist band and heavily asterisked pro cycling career. Landis is Floyd Landis. He did what Froome just did but way back when. Like Lazarus from the ashes. A subsequent positive test rather spoilt the occasion.*

descriptors. The riders, dulled in the final stages through sheer attrition, were hanging on.

As a pre-emptive strike against the perspective police I might add that no-one died (though Thibaut Pinot had a good go). It's just a bike race, and as far as we know participation was consensual. Though the human rights records of Bahrain and the UAE make it wise to keep a close eye on the likes of Pozzovivo and Aru.

But Rome, and stage twenty-one, will see pink water flowing through the Trevi fountain and Chris Froome will be the holder of all three Grand Tours.

Anyone who says they saw *that* coming seventy-two hours ago is a liar.

stage 21: ROME

I f you were settling in for a game of Giro Bingo today while the riders lapped Rome on the final stage, you won't have been disappointed.

Chris Froome on a pink bike – check. Sprint finish described as "gladiatorial" – check. Froome as the new "Roman Emperor" – check. Team Sky coasting across the finish line band-of-brothers style – check. Limited edition Rapha kit for the occasion – check. Lingering shot of the trophy engraver, mid-engrave – check.

After the punishment of the mountains during the final week this was a different bike race; the time-honoured change of pace for a processional final stage. When the inevitable sprint came, Viviani's Quick Step lead out train resembled HTC Highroad back in the glory days of Cavendish, on the Champs Elysees, in 2009.

Hitting the final kilometre Viviani had three teammates in linear formation. They were delivering him with precision for his adoring public. He launched, on the shiny city cobbles of the finishing straight, hopping, skipping and slithering in the search for traction. And Sam Bennett, working to a different script, powered past for the win.

Final Score: Viviani 4, Bennett 3.

And, as it turned out, the 2018 Giro *wasn't* the occasion when the law of averages kicked in and the leader of a Grand Tour hit the deck on the final stage, broke a leg, and failed to finish (it'll happen one year).

In celebration of both his Pink Jersey and the integrity of his tibia you would hope Froome hit the nightlife of Rome post-stage, for a massive pizza and half a crate of Peroni.

No doubt the bars were recce'd thoroughly six months ago; bespoke, wind-tunnel tested evening wear was worn; and the whole team were forced to warm down on turbo trainers before they could pass out in their hotel rooms.

Perfectly choreographed, beautifully executed fun. A pub crawl, Team Sky style.

Dress code: pink.

giro d'italia 2018 final standings

1st Chris FROOME (GBR: Team Sky)

2nd Tom DUMOULIN (NED: Team Sunweb) +46"

3rd Miguel Angel LOPEZ (COL: Astana) +4'57"

Points: Elia VIVIANI (ITA: Quick-Step Floors)

King of the Mountains: Chris FROOME (GBR: Team Sky)

Young Rider: Miguel Angel LOPEZ (COL: Astana)

Tour de France

There are many ways to describe the Tour de France. It's a carnival, a celebration, and an exercise in corporate hospitality. It's a great rolling behemoth. It rumbles around France each year, gathering up everything in its path and depositing it, rearranged, for someone else to tidy up.

For the cycling fan it's the way in. The gateway drug to the hard stuff. You can dabble in the Tour de France in a way you can't with the Giro. The Giro requires commitment, effort, and paraphernalia, where the Tour is a quick buzz before you wander off, none the worse for wear, to get on with your life.

Cinematically speaking it's a glossy blockbuster, unchallenging and fun while it lasts. Mainstream. Showbiz. Occasional deep moments of reflection followed by a bad guy in a clown suit abseiling down the Eiffel Tower.

It's often said, simply, that "the Tour is the Tour." With a shrug and a *what can you do?* It's bigger than all of us. Arguing with the Tour would be like arguing with Mont Blanc.

But for the winner – of the race, but even a stage – it's a life changer. You retire happy. It's an income, a book deal, and a place in the pantheon. To rub up along Coppi, Anquetil and Merckx. Indurain, Contador, and Froome.

The 2018 edition covered three-thousand-three-hundred kilometres over its traditional three weeks. Through twenty-one stages we began in the Vendéee, before a tour of Brittany, a lottery on the cobbles of northern France, and the usual mix of mountains, sprints, crashes and carnage.

The set-piece TV spectacular was, as it often is, the summit finish to Alpe d'Huez on stage twelve; a telegenic cauldron of hairpins and baying fans. The closest pro cycling gets to an arena.

The Tour also gave us a frankly obscenely entertaining cameo from Frenchman Julian Alaphilippe, who took the King of the Mountains competition and turned it into a piece of performance art; all joyous attacking and bravado, a study in body language and facial hair.

A man so obviously enjoying himself, and entertaining us, it was difficult not to rise to his every appearance on the TV screen and applaud.

But is Le Tour the best?

The most entertaining?

The hardest?

The most dramatic?

It matters not.

Because the Tour is the Tour, and it doesn't care what you think.

stages 1-3: VENDÉE AT A TIME

stage 1

I t begins, as the Tour always does, with a number of questions which require an answer.

By what method will Richie Porte contrive to lose time against his rivals? On what stage will Chris Froome hit the deck with his own, personal, single-cyclist crash? How will Movistar resolve their unwieldly triple team leadership issue? Who is this year's big beast in the sprinting jungle? What mood will Mark Cavendish be in?

Rather than have these questions answered in slow-burn-stage-by-stage-tension-raising fashion, this year we've got them all out of the way early.

For around one-hundred-and-eighty of today's two-hundred-kilometre opening stage between Noirmoutier-en-l'Ile and Fontenay-le-Comte, all was following the formula set by the pancake flat profile: an early breakaway formed, happy to soak up the TV coverage, before being reeled back in for a quick, flat, sprinters showdown at the finish. And then, as sometimes happens in the Tour, a quiet day became suddenly noisy and slightly panic-stricken.

Questions, in the blink of an eye, became answers.

Richie Porte was caught up in a crash with ten kilometres to go, leaving him the wrong side of the race and losing a minute to his rivals. So that didn't take long. Froome then attempted to share a thin strip of Tarmac with perhaps the widest of all the cyclists – Marcel Kittel – and ended up in a field covered in grass stains[28]. He leapt back up, but the race barrelled on and he finished in the Porte group.

And, as we know, "the Porte group" is not the place to be. You may want to consider your options. Perhaps you could check in with the commentary team to see how they've labelled the situation?

"Hi chaps…quick question: Just wondered what you're calling this group. The chasers? The groups of contenders? What…the Porte group? Oh Shit!"

Porte, you see, is a brilliant, consistent, bike-race-winning pro cyclist, but the biggest race of all – le Tour – is his bête noire. His nemesis. He turns up each year looking lean, every inch the winner in waiting. Then he falls off. Avoid Porte, and the chances of you getting tangled up in his misfortune are reduced.

---

[28]*To emerge from a field, covered in grass stains, hints at naughtiness. It depends where on the body the grass stains are found, I suppose, and whether other, equally grass-stained people are involved. Either way, it's not a good look for a pro cyclist.*

Don't be in "the Porte group" would be my advice.

But others, too, shed precious time. Movistar's leader (perhaps, depending on who you ask, and on what day) Nairo Quintana dashed both his wheels against a traffic island in the final kilometres. He hung around roadside, waiting for spares, while Landa and Valverde (also leaders of Movistar, depending on who you ask, and on what day) rattled onwards to the finish.

Footage of the miniature Colombian watching the race sail by was poignant; a small boy, abandoned on a school trip and trying to remember the lost child protocol. I wanted to give him a little cuddle and take him to the nearest police station.

None of this drama, though, prevented our sprint finish. Belgian winning machine Quick Step Floors, one powerhouse rider at a time, delivered Colombian Fernando Gaviria, the next cab off that rank marked "sprinting sensation," into prime position. He unleashed an effort which held off Peter Sagan and comfortably crushed Kittel.

Convincing.

And Cavendish?

Pre-race he was philosophical, even genial, like an elder statesman who's crunched the numbers and doesn't like his chances. Post-race he cuddled and canoodled his tiny fortnight-old son for the cameras. He made a quip about being left holding the baby. It was lovely stuff.

When I finally write "Parenting for pro-cyclists - a guide" Cav will get rave reviews. He'll be on the cover. A shining example for the next generation of tunnel-visioned Alpha males. But as a bike racer I like my Mark Cavendish to be tetchy, grumpy, and operating on a short fuse. Scowling and snarling. Picking fights.

Can Cav the caring dad really win bike races?

The last words on stage one go to Porte, who summed things up with: "It's the first day of the Tour. It's not ideal."

No, Richie. But then it never is, is it?

stage 2

It's far too early to say whether this edition of the Tour de France might turn out to be a classic. It does, however, already include one of the pre-requisites for classic status: a single rider, suffering excessively, for no practical reason.

Whatever is going on between the riders competing for jerseys the back story provided by the also-rans is crucial. Pain and heroic resistance are irresistible.

Imagine the extras milling around in the background of Downton Abbey being forced to do it with cracked collar bones and dislodged vertebrae. You're more likely to watch, right?

In 2013, for example, Geraint Thomas rode almost an entire Tour with a broken pelvis. It was probably excruciating. But the golden rule of the Tour is that you don't abandon unless you absolutely have to; it's too important, and prestigious. As a trade-off, the rider involved acquires the ultimate must-have accessory for the image conscious pro cyclist; a hardman anecdote from the highest level of the sport.

Broken fingers and wrists will work, collarbones are common yet classic, but backs, hips, and necks are where the real kudos lie.

This year, taking on the mantle to defy tremendous pain for the benefit of a global TV audience, is American rider Lawson Craddock

In crashing on stage one he fractured his scapula – the shoulder blade, essentially – *and* received a whole needleful of stitches in his head. He battled to the end of the stage, went off to hospital for treatment, and took the start line today to get busy building his own little Power Point presentation for the after-dinner circuit.

Each time the TV director cut to the back of the peloton there he was; hanging on, dangling off occasionally, but holding fast. And he's getting pleasingly creative with the role. For each stage he survives he's pledged to donate a crisp hundred to charity, and he's drumming up support for others to do the same.

Cycling celebrity awaits.

When the cameras weren't panning back to check on Craddock during today's stage between Mouilleron-Saint-Germain and La Roche-Sur-Yon they were cutting between crashes, mechanical failures, punctures, and all manner of mishap and misfortune. The most crucial of these took down early race leader Fernando Gaviria in the final kilometres and held up most of the rest of the peloton, leaving a select group to try and beat Sagan in the sprint.

They couldn't.

Everyone's favourite Slovak had plenty of committed teammates on full-alert, and *he* now wears the leader's Yellow Jersey. To wear on top of his Green Jersey. Which he pulls on over his National Champions Jersey. That covers the Rainbow Jersey denoting his World Champion status. And was that his twenty-five-metre swimming badge I saw sewn onto the leg of his bib-shorts?

I'm pretty sure he has to wear all the jerseys he's earned at once; that's how it works, right?

Apart from Craddock, and Sagan, there was one more star of the show today: on his three hundred and fiftieth Tour stage veteran Frenchman Sylvain Chavanel was in crowd-pleasing mood.

In the early three-man break he eventually went clear alone, not to win the stage, but to bask in the adulation of a sun-kissed French public. At one point he rode alone through a tunnel of fans, arms outstretched crucifix style, high-fiving every man, woman and child.

Lovely stuff.

We also got the eminently quotable stat that as of today Chavanel has spent over a year, in total, on his bike and riding the Tour de France in his eighteen editions to date. Depending on your perspective that's either a glorious testimony to a sporting life, or a monument to utter futility. I take the first option.

Chapeau Chava!

As for Lawson Craddock, he rolled home safely (if painfully) and lives to fight on. Did I mention his race number is "13"?

Unlucky for some.

stage 3

The Team Time Trial, as a discipline, is clinical. It's about precision. Pointy helmets and mirrored visors are essential.

A well-drilled team packed with on-form riders who are comfortable oversharing their physique in a skin-suit will swish and swoosh around the course; taking turns, tucking in, and maintaining pleasingly perpendicular positions on the bike. A team with one or two weak links, or even good riders on bad days, will find themselves – and I apologise in advance for my use of a technical cycling term – all over the shop.

At one point on stage three the camera cut to Belgian super-team Quick Step who were scattered asunder, up and down the road, in pieces. That they managed to pull their dignity back together suggests they weren't *quite* all over the shop, but they were certainly browsing different aisles and working from their own shopping lists.

One look at Team Sky, in their menace of black and white and counting three current national time-trial champions in their ranks, and you knew they *were* quick. Their skin suits a little shinier, their backs a little flatter, their rear wheels a little, erm...wheel-ier!?

They couldn't have been *more* clinical had they dressed in white coats and held a drop-in surgery at the nearest health centre.

Which makes the stage win today for BMC Racing all the more impressive; another team that know their way around a TTT. I mean, they ride Swiss bikes for goodness sake. Clockwork precision is clearly at work (other national stereotypes are available).

All of which ultimately, in perhaps the most Grand Tour-y of all Grand Tour disciplines, put a one-day specialist in the Yellow Jersey in the form of granite-jawed Belgian Greg Van Avermaet. Deposing another one-day specialist, Peter Sagan. And pipping a third – Philippe Gilbert – whose Quick Step team, to bring to a close a rather drawn-out analogy, managed to reconvene at the checkout and pay for their shopping using the same corporate credit card.

Talking of Van Avermaet, the stat wranglers were quick to confirm that he's the first reigning Olympic champion to wear yellow at the Tour de France. I had it in my mind that British decathlete (and Olympic champ) Daley Thompson rode as a mountain domestique for Bernard Hinault's La Vie Clare team and briefly held yellow back in1985, but a quick Google confirms I may have made that up for comedy purposes.

It's funny what tricks the memory can play, eh?

We know Van Avermaet is the Olympic champ, of course, because he rides the gold bike to remind us. Fair enough. He's proud of his achievement and he wants to display that fact. Also, the bike manufacturer wants to sell more bikes. No problem.

I would suggest, however, that if they choose to use the Olympic "brand" (eugh...wash my mouth out!) they should do so comprehensively. The Olympic Committee should get their money's worth.

The Olympics, after all, is about the strive to be: "Faster, Higher, Stronger, and with increased visibility in a fragmented marketplace."

GVA could surely still contribute his share in the TTT line-up with a gold medal dangling around his neck, holding aloft the Olympic flame for Tokyo 2020 with one hand and steering with the other.

In fact, as the peloton rolls out from La Baule on stage four tomorrow he could casually turn left as the race turns right and pedal off alone, with a flourish, on a mission to spread the Olympic message (whilst, conveniently, also promoting BMC bikes).

What a marketing ploy that could be.

stages 4-6: BRITTANY

stage 4

For three stages of this Tour de France my will-power had prevailed. I've grown to like having a job, a wife, and kids who, if pushed, could pick me out of a line-up. I was in no mood to jeopardise that. All was going well.

And then I stumbled accidentally[29] across a Tweet from purveyors of real time Tour data @letourdata and disappeared into a parallel universe.

Once the deep-dive into data has begun escape becomes impossible. Who knows where it will end: Divorce? Alcoholism? Fathers 4 Justice? Like an addict, given a hit, real life melts away to be replaced by granular graphs of Tom Dumoulin's speed data, rider

---

[29]*Accidentally in as much as I was on Twitter, had pressed the search icon, and was casually typing the words Tour de France data.*

profiles in the form of radar charts, and final kilometre sprint heat-maps.

It makes Strava seem like mere gateway data. A sweet-shop bag of weed to the crystal-meth favoured by the grown-ups.

The reason I found myself idly crunching the numbers was that it was a quiet day. One of those dull Grand Tour stages that acts as vital context for the exciting bits.

The break formed early, pleasingly composed of a two French and two Belgian riders; perhaps in honour of the evening's football World Cup semi-final between the two countries? A state of play that could only have been improved by the *actual* Romelu Lukaku and the *literal* Paul Pogba heading up the road to join them, mid-race, in a doomed bid for a stage win.

The break built a lead of eight minutes before the peloton started the reeling-in process. We had a little bit of will-they-won't-they tension towards the end, and then a four-hundred metre finishing straight where an entire gallop of lead-out men came to the fore, snarling and flexing in service of their sprinters.

Because a flat(ish) stage with a four-hundred metre finishing straight will *always* end with a sprint. The only way to flag this fact more obviously would have been to give the lead-out men a baton to pass to their fast finisher, and have Sally Gunnell skulk just beyond the finishing line poised for an awkward interview[30].

Fernando Gaviria won, for the record, pipping Sagan to the line. His Quick Step team doing their now familiar job of totally and utterly bossing matters. The Colombian now has a fifty-percent Tour de France strike rate (two wins from four stage starts). If he maintains that for a whole career worth of Tours de France he could end up with as many as a hundred and five stage wins (the mighty Eddy Merckx currently holds the record with thirty-four).

Sounds unlikely, I know, but we live in a world where Donald Trump can be President, playing computer games is considered a sport, and my local café has a "house hummus."

In that context, let's not rule anything out.

As if to underline a low-key day, for the first time in this year's race none of the main contenders lost any time and the Yellow Jersey stayed where it was (across the torso of the mighty Greg Van Avermaet).

stage 5

Stage five, on the roads of Brittany, offered us *two* varieties of terrain: an uphill variety, and a downhill variety. Secret variety

---

[30]*That one's for you, 90's British athletics fans.*

number three – flat roads – were deemed surplus to requirements. Hills were to be ridden. Polka dots were to be earned.

Interestingly, the route profile was designed to perfectly resemble the up and down waves of Bernard Hinault's furrowed Breton brow; a nice touch from the race organisers in the home region of the five-time Tour winner. Achieving this, of course, took some considerable effort – the route wasn't finalised until a couple of weeks before the Grand Depart.

To ensure total accuracy I understand the race organisers sent a delegation around to Hinault's house, comprising an experienced cycling journalist and a professional make-up artist with a big bucket of plaster of Paris.

The irascible Frenchman was then asked to consider his next public utterance on the Chris Froome/Salbutamol situation - the brow instantly furrowed, the plaster was slapped on with speed and precision, and a cast was made to display Hinault's exact physical response. From there, the dimensions of the model brow were fed into some clever GPS software, et voila: today's parcours was the result.

Rumours that the organisers of the Giro d'Italia are considering something similar using Mario Cipollini's naked torso are, as yet, unconfirmed. Rumours that this suggestion was made by Cipollini himself are almost certainly true.

But knowing that today's stage was based on Bernie's craggy bonce wasn't enough; It was the kind of stage that we also like to compare to something else so we can mentally map it within the standard range of pro cycling terrain. We want to understand where it sits on the spectrum between pan-flat parade and five-col Alpine summit finish.

Ultimately, we're talking a mini Liege-Bastogne-Liege; slightly shorter, with better weather, and more entertainment. Also without the reverence for all things Belgian cycling; a reverence that is *always* maintained *even* when the race is clearly travelling through an industrial estate, before turning left onto a dreary housing estate, ready to negotiate the next set of roadworks against a backdrop of electricity pylons.

No offence Belgium, but Brittany is prettier.

Even when it resembles Bernard Hinault.

The seven-man break that went clear today were tasked with mopping up King of the Mountain points en route – one of these guys would end the day in the Polka Dot Jersey. Sylvain Chavanel, he of the record eighteen consecutive Tour appearances, was a man on a mission.

I like to imagine that, along with being in control of the break, he took charge of conversation, too; all misty eyed, no doubt, and regaling his companions with nearly two decades worth of Tour de France anecdotes.

"Hey guys," he'd be saying, "did I ever tell you I wore the Yellow Jersey twice in 2010?"

"Erm...yeah, I think you did Chava."

"So, it was Stage two when I won it first, in Belgium...great day, actually...bit cloudy if I remember rightly...anyway, me and Fabian were just chatting when suddenly Alberto appeared..."

eyes roll

As it happened Chavanel eventually talked himself out of energy and Latvian Tom Skujins wrapped up the Polka Dot scavenger hunt. For the stage finale, with the break done and dusted, we were treated to a showdown between the one-day specialists and the climbers who can finish fast.

We're talking Sagan, Van Avermaet, Gilbert, Nibali, Martin, Valverde, Alaphilippe and, impressively, Sonny Colbrelli. It was like northern Europe in April but without the cobbles and the cow-shit. Sagan won, like Sagan does.

If only Bernard Hinault could've mounted the podium at the end and punched someone in the face for old time's sake. It would've capped off the day beautifully. I can only assume he was otherwise engaged. Back home on his farm, perhaps? Propped up at the kitchen table, brow furrowed, and elbow deep in the fine print of the UCI Chris Froome/Salbutamol Ruling.

stage 6

In modern pro cycling the big budget teams will spend time and money recce'ing climbs and other potentially important stretches of road. Sometimes on Google maps, but often in person. It's a very labour-intensive way of securing a small advantage for your riders.

You could argue it *dis*advantages riders from lesser teams on smaller budgets who can't afford to send a lackey trotting around Europe looking closely at Tarmac for a living. But that argument is a blind alley. Big budget equals more advantages. C'est la vie.

Helpfully, today, the race organisers took pity on the poor relations of the peloton and allowed them to recce the major climb of the day during the *actual* race.

With around fifteen kilometres to go they climbed the Mûr de Bretagne, taking notes and making observations as they went. They then looped around, and back, and up the Mûr again. This time for real, and with a finishing line at the top. What an egalitarian solution to the aching financial chasm inherent in the pro cycling business model.

Vive La France!

But look who won.

Dan Martin of UAE Team Emirates (and therefore with the financial backing of a selection of Emirates). Not a sniff for the poor relations. Perhaps they weren't concentrating first time up the Mûr.

Instead of doing their homework they were busy playing with their phones, or flicking each other's ears, or whatever else cash-strapped pro cyclists do when they're pressed into action in the service of a heavy-handed school-based analogy.

Today the race was tailor made for the Irishman. The stage was Ardennes-esque in its use of short, sharp climbs, and Martin has got winning history in the Belgian Ardennes. He went at the final kilometre like a bored hamster at a box-fresh toilet roll.

With two hundred metres to go French pup Pierre Latour had him all but caught, but like a long-limbed cartoon boxer the Irishman stretched out a metaphorical arm and placed a boxing glove on Latour's forehead to hold him at bay.

It was a savage finish, all gaping mouth and flailing limbs.

Classic Dan Martin.

stages 7-9: CATHEDRALS, COBBLES AND COWSHIT

stage 7

A long, flat stage is all about the set-piece sprint finish. We can all get on with our day – a nice bit of lunch, maybe a spot of work if we have to – before gathering around the telly late afternoon for the final ten kilometres. This is where the action happens. And yet, in full knowledge of this fact, the historic finish town of Chartres missed a trick.

Sure, it was exciting enough, as the big sprinter's teams threw the kitchen sink at the slightly uphill drag to the finish, but it could have been so much more. It could have been Biblical. They could have really pushed the boat (or should that be Arc) out.

Chartres has a famous Cathedral, right? So, stick the Flamme Rouge[31] a kilometre from the pulpit and have Sagan, Gaviria, Kittel and Greipel sprint in through the main entrance, down the aisles, and lunge for a finish line cast in the holy light of one hundred and seventy-six stained-glass windows. Now *that* would be a spectacle.

Chartres Cathedral, religion fans, is a Roman Catholic institution, and I can't help thinking that for the prestige of a Tour de France finish Papal approval for my suggested cathedral-based finale wouldn't have been be a problem – Popes have been known to regularly receive (and revere) pro cyclists down the years.

Back in January 2018, in fact, Pope Francis invited Peter Sagan to the Vatican where this great man, beloved by millions of devoted followers across the globe, presented the head honcho of the Catholic Church with a rainbow jersey and special edition bike.[32]

A Sagan-friendly sprint through Chartres Cathedral is the least his Pope-ship could do in return.

Just imagine the atmosphere. A couple of thousand adrenaline-fuelled cycling fans could really make use of those twelfth century acoustics. Maybe Eurosport's Carlton Kirby could've dressed in full Catholic regalia and delivered his frantic commentary like a sermon?

---

[31]*The flamme rouge is the one kilometre to go banner. These days, it tends to be left unlit. Health and safety, I suppose.*

[32]*When asked what they talked about, Sagan told reporters (with a glint in his eye): "Pope Francis asked me to pray for him."*

Alas, it wasn't to be. The powers that be went for the more conventional finishing terrain of a road, outdoors.

In the final stages, as Sagan and Gaviria watched each other like hawks, Dutchman Dylan Groenewegen unleashed a devastating finishing burst – all biceps and shoulders – and very nearly pulled his own bike to pieces for an imposing win. Much more of that and he, too, will find himself at the Vatican, donating yet more pro cycling memorabilia to the Pontiff's private collection.

stage 8

Dylan Groenewegen is one of those sportspeople who looks like they've been destined to excel from the moment they left their mother's womb. There he was, back in 1993, all blotchy and wrapped in blankets. Media-trained and brand aware. Giving an effortless on-message post-birth interview.

These days he is clean cut and chiselled, and apparently undaunted by the stage he finds himself on. As if winning massive bike races is the most natural thing in the world.

On stage eight's fast finish into Amiens he timed his late burst to beat Demare, Sagan, Gaviria, and Greipel. Two stage wins in two days. Calm. Unruffled. Not a hair out of place. Blotch-free.

Amiens itself is one of those places which exude familiarity. Whether you've been there or not it'll undoubtedly have popped up on your radar; perhaps you've navigated around it on a drive south, made a mental note on Remembrance Day as a town of the Somme, or stumbled across it in a Sebastian Faulkes novel (you little smarty pants).

I feel I could probably describe the place to you in reasonable detail. I could talk at length about the character of the people, explaining what makes them tick, before giving you a potted history of the Cathedral and heading home to cook you the local delicacy.

I couldn't say for certain, though, whether I've ever *actually* been there.

Maybe it was fitting, then, that such a ubiquitous French town be the star attraction on Bastille Day; although truth be told, as Bastille Days go, it was a quiet one. It passed by with an air of you-know-tomorrow-is-the-cobbles, right? In hindsight they probably should have drafted in Faulkes to craft one of his compelling narratives to carry things along.

It would be overdoing it to suggest we've spent eight days of this Tour de France twiddling our thumbs and waiting for cobbles, but they have rather loomed over proceeding thus far.

Friends and acquaintances – otherwise uninterested in pro cycling - ask about the race. They know the Tour de France is currently happening and they're curious. Pretty quickly they wonder why I appear to be talking about cobbles, and with such fervour.

Sprints, they get.

Mountains make sense.

But cobbles?

I simply suggest they tune in tomorrow.

stage 9

Stage nine – yes, on the cobbles of northern France - was always going to be about survival. Could the various Yellow Jersey contenders, flimsy mountain climbers almost to a man, limit their losses and avoid catastrophe in the domain of the one-day specialists?

The answer to that questions was, barring a few unfortunates, yes.

How, is another matter entirely.

I would love to talk you through the incidents and accidents that led to John Degenkolb winning a sprint against Greg van Avermaet and Yves Lampaert, whilst the main contenders finished largely together and intact just a short distance behind. But short of sitting in front of a complete re-run of today's race and narrating it in real time, that's going to be tricky.

So, to sum up, what happened on today's stage between Arras and Roubaix was everything. Absolutely everything.

All of the cycling things happened.

Degenkolb was emotional at the finish, looking like a man who'd narrowly survived the big set piece shoot-out at the end of an action movie. He was only a tight white vest away from Bruce Willis at his most knowingly heroic.

This is a man, Degenkolb, who back in 2015 was entering genuine superstar territory. A spectacular Milan-San Remo/Paris Roubaix double had made sure of that. Two monuments[33] in a career would secure near-legend status for most riders, which rather adds context to the German's two monuments in three weeks. That's one every ten and half days, on average.

Impressive.

And then, in early 2016, while winter training in Spain with his teammates, came a crash caused by an erratic holidaymaker in a hire car. Badly injured, and nearly losing a finger, the season was a write-off.

The following year, 2017, was patchy at best. Questions were being asked. Knowing glances being exchanged. All of which requires us to file a Tour stage win on the cobbles under "R" for redemption.

Which, co-incidentally, could easily be the title of the next Bruce Willis movie.

The emotion of Degenkolb, after all of that, was understandable.

---

[33]*The Monuments are the oldest, hardest, and most revered of all the one-day classics. They comprise Milan-San Remo, Paris Roubaix, the Tour of Flanders, Liege-Bastogne-Liege, and Il Lombardia. Win a monument, and a career is complete.*

As it was for Richie Porte; everyone's favourite Tasmanian ended the race, as he does so often, sitting roadside, teary-eyed and clutching an apparent broken bone. You'd have to have a cobble for a heart not to feel for the guy.

Chris Froome had a crash (of course) but managed to fight his way through in the company of the main group. Mikel Landa hit the Tarmac hard whilst taking a slurp from his drinks bottle and also, slightly implausibly, after seeing him lying prone in a tangle of bikes of riders, managed to haul himself back into contact.

But the man of the day – apart from Degenkolb - was Romain Bardet. The French hope. A slight, Will 'o' the Wisp of a rider who had clearly climbed the wrong side out of bed and smashed a mirror whilst failing to negotiate a black cat. I counted four (or was it five, or maybe ten?) mechanical issues during the stage.

The final one – a front wheel puncture with but a few kilometres to go – left him alone on the road, with neither team mates to help nor a group of fellow riders to hook up with. Any chances he had of winning the Tour were, at that moment, in the balance.

The cameras zoomed in for a closer look. He shook his head momentarily, flashing a look that seemed to say: "Pffssshhh, these cobbles 'eh...what a lot of fun and games this is."

At least that's the family friendly version. His actual thoughts would've been more grown-up, including words beginning with letters like 'f' and 's'...maybe even 'c'!? Perhaps questioning the parentage of whoever had proposed the bright idea of including the savagery of cobbles within the civility of the Tour de France.

How he managed to chase back and catch up with the main group of contenders is lost to the director's cut of today's stage. Conspiracy theorists will mutter vaguely about "assistance" for the French hero from camera bikes and team cars. .

Whatever.

If Bardet comes back to win the whole thing that, right there, was the very cusp of the brink.

stages 10-12: THE ALPS

stage 10

"There's a time and place for cobbles in pro cycling," said rent-a-quote Mitchelton-Scott boss Matt White, as if to back-up Romain Bardet's mid-race musings during Sunday's incident strewn road to Roubaix, "...and that's in April."

Stage nine had provided just *too much* excitement for some people. For the first eight stages the contrary consensus of opinion had been growing. Sure, we had sprint finishes, a team time trial, and Bernard Hinault's furrowed Breton brow, but we also had long kilometres of not very much. *Not enough* excitement was the general feeling.

And so, on the basis that we appear to be witnessing the Goldilocks Tour this year, today's first foray into the Alps was poised to deliver levels of excitement that were *just right*.

Marc Madiot, team boss of Groupama-FDJ, had likened Tour Director Christian Prudhomme's job to that of a movie director; piecing together a storyline using scenes from a menu of options.

The cobbles of stage nine were the special-effect-laden action sequence. The script for stage ten, between Annecy and le Grand Bornand, was clear. It was to be the day when Greg Van Avermaet – one-day specialist and current wearer of the Yellow Jersey – would be sent tumbling down the General Classification by the climbers.

The big man[34] had other ideas.

In an early plot twist GVA managed to infiltrate the day's breakaway along with twenty-one other riders. From there he fought, and battled, and clung, and...well, *extended* his lead.

Consolidated his Yellow Jersey.

Cyclists today, eh? Attention seekers. They can't just learn their lines and play their part.

But to focus on Van Avermaet is to ignore one of his breakaway companions and *the* star of the day: French rider Julian Alaphilippe. The record books suggest that this was the first Tour de France victory of his career which, frankly, I simply don't believe.

---

[34]*Big man, that is, for a pro cyclist. Were he stood next to me, an average man, he would look tiny.*

If you'd asked any cycling fan, pre-stage, if Alaphilippe has ever won a Tour stage they'd have made the puzzled eyebrows and probably got quite animated:

"Yeah...course he has. Pfffhhh! You complete idiot. Moron! What is WRONG with you!"

At which point you'd be backing away gently, regretting asking a psychopath for their view on a bike race, whilst tentatively admiring the vehemence of their support for Alaphilippe. Pushed on the detail from a safe distance (about twenty yards, I suppose) they'd have fussed and blustered:

"Well, erm...there was that time, err..."

But they wouldn't have backed down. Alaphilippe is *made* for Tour stage wins. If I close my eyes and think *really hard* I conjure a mental image of at least three of them and yet the record keepers, for some reason, beg to differ. No wonder he looked super-motivated to set the record straight and claim his first Tour stage win since (accurate) records began.

And, to cap it off, it was an absolute beauty.

From that early break he was out in front from the start. As the group whittled away around him he looked perky and light, and with thirty kilometres to go he attacked solo; devouring Alps like a hungry child going at an airport Toblerone. And he wasn't sharing.

By the summit of the final climb – the Col de la Colombiere, around fifteen kilometres from the finish – he was well clear and one swooping descent away from the win. It was never in doubt.

I'm even prepared to forgive him the goatee beard.

For now.

stage 11

The Tour de France, for the riders, is death by a thousand cuts. A drip-drip of hourly, daily, weekly suffering which leaves us, in the end, with a winner. One bloke who's less broken than all the others.

Stage eleven, though, was something else; less death by a thousand cuts and more whack round the back of the head with a shovel. A short, sharp, blunt instrument, if such a thing could exist. One hundred and eight kilometres, four summits, in a blur.

As Grand Tour stages go that's as short as they come.

The road from Albertville to La Rosiere was *sure* (barring another virtuoso display from van Avermaet) to give us our first "proper" Yellow Jersey of the 2018 Tour; by which I mean a race leader who can climb and defend a lead in the mountains. A rider with GC ambitions. A team leader. Someone a bit less Belgian and a bit more British, Spanish, or Italian.

Team Sky have got two of those (Thomas and Froome), while Movistar decided to bring three (Quintana, Landa and Valverde). Is that one leader and two spares? Or two leaders and one spare?

Cruelly, it's starting to resemble three spares.

Either way, it was time for powder, previously kept dry, to be, erm...made wet? Cards were to be shown and cats released from bags.

On the final climb to La Rosiere the pack was well and truly shuffled. For Movistar Valverde huffed, Landa puffed, and Quintana "did a Quintana"; he sat in the wheels, neither attacking nor defending, just being. Because, for Team Sky, La Rosiere was the scene of another trademark show of utter dominance.

From the foot of the climb, with at least five riders on the front, they drove the pace. Once the main bunch had been given a thorough seeing-to Geraint Thomas burst clear, leaving team-mate Froome to cat-and-mouse a while with Nibali, Roglic, Bardet, and Quintana.

Thomas then bridged across to Tom Dumoulin, who was busy time-trialling up the mountain (and the General Classification), and the Welshman sat on his wheel and borrowed his considerable slipstream. Froome, meanwhile, left his little group of pals and bridged across, leaving Thomas to burst clear *again*, sweep past a flagging Mikel Nieve, and win the stage.

It was a beautifully choreographed set-piece of controlled violence. Imagine Torvil and Dean in a knife fight. Are you doing that? Great.

Well done you. It's fun isn't it? In your version is Jane the aggressor while Christopher cowers out of harm's way? Yes, mine too.

Anyway. Now forget that, and imagine Geraint Thomas wearing the Yellow Jersey with Chris Froome in second. Less fun, more accurate. That's how it looks now at the Tour, the British team dominating the race.

Movistar and their three prongs were left in bits. The same applies to everyone else. Pick a leader from any other team and, bar Dumoulin, they lost time. For Bardet, Nibali, Quintana and Roglic, it was tens of seconds. For Adam Yates, Valverde, Landa, Jungels, and other unfortunates, it was minutes.

The spoils belong to Sky and the General Classification has been bludgeoned into some kind of recognisable form. And that form is Sky-shaped.

stage 12

Prior to today's stage twelve, Steven Kruijswijk was known for two things: as the man with shoulders like coat hangers, and for his performance at the 2016 Giro d'Italia. On that occasion he wore the leader's jersey for a couple of imperious weeks before crashing dramatically into a snow drift and chucking it all away.

He "did a Simon Yates" before it was fashionable.

And, I might add, he did it more photogenically. Where Yates opted this year for the simplistic sinking-into-a-bottomless-pit-ofexhaustion approach, Kruijswijk used a massive snowdrift as a prop in his demise.

Style points.

But now, finally, he has a third string to that bow of memories (whatever the hell one of those might be).

Alpe d'Huez is known for many things, one of which being the massive party that takes place at the hairpin bend known as "Dutch corner". So to be a Dutch cyclist (as Kruijswijk is) and lead a big mountain stage, clear of the peloton, and through the hairpin bend known as "Dutch Corner" alone, is definitely a bit of a moment. Its career defining stuff.

A sport like pro cycling, which thrives on the side-stories, does this kind of thing better than any other sport. If the fans had built a fake snowdrift and Kruijswijk had staged a mock made-for-TV tumble for the hell of it we could've all packed up, gone home, and found some other way to fill our time.

That would've been the pinnacle.

But Kruijswik is the consummate pro. He elected not to fake his own crash and instead cracked on to attempt the win. Unfortunately, his mighty hail-Mary seventy-kilometre attack was cruelly reeled in with just a handful to go. Those vast shoulders slumped, and he clung on to salvage a mere good day from the ashes of a flippin' heroic one.

While he was doing that Froome, Bardet, Thomas, Dumoulin and Landa were strung out, five-abreast, and jockeying for position in the closing stages. With the rest of the field scattered across this great climb like the dregs of a party, these five were left to duke it out, mano y mano y mano y mano y mano.

The road swept through its final bends and Geraint Thomas, having ridden a canny climb, responding to attacks and choosing wheels, opened up a hitherto unseen high-altitude uphill sprint. Dumoulin tracked him for second. Bardet, Froome and Landa made up the quintet.

Post-stage Thomas, having consolidated his Yellow Jersey, continued to give it the genial jack-the-lad, praising Froome and toeing the team-leader line. As TV's Ned Boulting noted yesterday, regarding Team Sky's internal politics:

"At the very least we have a situation."

Tomorrow, we all draw breath as the roads flatten out for a while. Bearing in mind that, through abandonments and time cuts, *literally* all the main sprinters are now out of the race (Cavendish, Kittel, Groenewegen, Gaviria, Greipel), we might not have seen the last of G's prowess in the sprint.

Three wins in a row, anyone?

stages 13-15: CROSS-COUNTRY TO CARCASSONNE

stage 13

Stage thirteen, long and hot, was your classic transitional stage. Get the riders across country from the Alps to the Pyrenees, take in a few chateaus for the tourist board – maybe linger over the occasional lavender field or orange grove – and deliver a flat-ish finish to placate the sprinters after the torment of the mountains.

Job done.

Problem was, and as previously mentioned, there was barely a sprinter to be found. The aforementioned mountains had seen to that.

Disappointing for us, the viewers, but opportunity knocked for Kristoff, Demare, and Degenkolb; fast finishers who excel when the pure sprinters have been shelled. Oh, and a certain Peter Sagan, who has been known to be spritely on occasion.

But as it unfolded, I found myself thinking of Cavendish.

The second most winning-est[35] cyclist in Tour de France history (thirty stages, and counting) had found himself, for a week and a bit in this year's Tour, off the pace. We had waited for him to come good, to no avail. His post-stage interviews revealed weakness and doubt. The usual bullishness was absent.

It was most un Cav-like; though to remain bullish after sprinting to twentieth position would've been delusional in the extreme.

And yet, as the lead-out trains gathered and the sprinters skipped from wheel to wheel on today's run-in to Valence I pictured Cav at home. Watching on, a selection of mini-Cav offspring clambering about him, and convinced that had he still been there he'd have won.

Spotting error and weakness in his rivals. Making mental notes on road furniture and wind direction. Scoffing at the way Demare's lead-out burnt too early, Kristoff mis-timed his lunge for the line, and Sagan edged them out for the win.

And despite the evidence before my eyes – his below-par 2018 form, his after-hours solo finish in the Alps (missing the time cut on stage eleven), and the doused fires of a doting father – I, too, can't *completely* convince myself he wouldn't have won today.

Vive le Cav!

---

[35]*Winny? Winnery? Winnering-est?*

When the Tour de France races up to the airfield at Mende, in the region of Occitanie, as it did today, exciting things happen. We always get a great race. That final climb – a few kilometres at ten percent or so – makes sure of it.

Back in 2015 it was British breakaway connoisseur Steve Cummings. He had us whooping, hollering, and doing a little jig in front of the telly (well, some of us, anyway) as he swept past the best that France had to offer (Bardet, and Pinot) thrillingly.

Today, Mende very kindly gave us *two* great races.

A large breakaway *eventually* established itself after some early stage crosswind-related shenanigans to build up a lead of more than twenty minutes over the peloton. Clearly the boffins at Sky, Sunweb, and Movistar had done their sums and concluded that no-one of any Tour de France winning consequence was in that leading group.

"Just ignore 'em Froomey," I imagine Sky henchman Luke Rowe saying, as if heading off a fight in an early-hours post-club taxi-rank, "they're not worth it."

Rowe dragged Froome off.

The break went on its merry way.

At the risk of killing the romance of the situation, I doubt any teams were having to do their sums. They have technology to do the figuring out for them. Some piece of software will have cross-tabbed the members of the break – identifiable by GPS signal – with their position on the General Classification, and given the main contenders the all clear.

Wouldn't it be great, though, if they got it wrong just once?

"We're OK chaps, let them go, we've had it checked and all the main guys are here with us. Look...there's Dumoulin and Bardet, Quintana is over there...I've seen Landa, he's hanging around somewhere with Roglic...and Geraint Thomas is...erm...wait, lads, where's G?"

"I think he's up the road, boss. Like, twenty minutes up the road."

"WHHHAAAAATTT! How's that happened? He's in a bright yellow jersey for f***'s sake!"

In race one, today, Alaphilippe, resplendent in King of the Mountain Polka Dots, appeared to be in full control. David Millar on ITV commentary was sure of it: "There's Alaphilippe, he's looking so in control. He's leaving it so late...that tells you how confident he is."

Too late, as it happened.

Too confident?

Astana's Spanish rider Omar Fraile held on for the win, and it wasn't pretty. Judging by the way he wrestled and wrangled his bike on the steep sections, pumping limbs like the poorly calibrated pistons of a steam engine, he may well be some distant relative of

Fabio Aru; the Italian for whom riding a bike is like some frenzied form of violence.

Race two saw Thomas and Froome, and Dumoulin, cat and mouse a while before consolidating a time gain on Romain Bardet. Not working together, exactly, but accepting a shared goal. Primoz Roglic was allowed to ride on and snatch a handful of seconds at the line.

Froome, throughout this, was predictably and disgracefully booed and abused by (some of) the crowd. On at least one occasion he had a liquid of some description thrown across him. Fans got very close and almost physical. He remains stoic and unbending in the face of this pitchfork mob mentality.

Whatever you think of Team Sky, and Froome himself, this does neither race nor watching public any credit. In post-race interviews the Sky rider refuses to engage with the subject, calmly batting away questions about his on-the-road treatment.

Perhaps he *should* talk about it?

Call out the idiots who threaten him when he's vulnerable, deep in effort, and in no position to defend himself?

Throw unidentified golden liquid on *them*...see how *they* like it.

Because if he doesn't, how else does this stop?

This race, in fact this sport, generates an awful lot of hot air. From fans, journalists, team bosses, riders, former riders; the list goes on. Several hours a day for three weeks leaves an awful lot of otherwise empty airtime, column inches, and hastily cobbled highlights packages to fill.

Down south, on the roads to Carcassonne, they also have their own, actual, literal hot air: The Vent d'Autan.

It is essentially a sea breeze, blowing in off the Mediterranean and funnelled by the geography of the French south-west. In the summer it blows hot and humid. For the breakaway on stage fifteen today it was one of the foes they had to battle. David Millar, ITV commentator and former pro, had his own take on life on today's break.

"If you're in the break you'll wish you were in the peloton, and if you're in the peloton you'll wish you were in the break. Unless you're Thomas de Gendt[36], who doesn't know the difference."

Today's stage, based on the profile, couldn't have been more obviously flagged as a day for the breakaway to win if they'd called it "The Thomas de Gendt memorial race."

He likes a break, does Thomas.

---

[36]*De Gendt is the most Medieval of all the cyclists. Both in name, and riding style. He essentially batters away at the pedals with no thought for his reserves of energy and how quickly they might be depleting. He's often in the break. He either dies or wins. He's Medieval.*

If you find yourself clear of the field and in the company of the bearded Belgian, you'd be forgiven for wavering on whether to be happy with your decision. De Gendt will pull hard, as he always does, and any respite will be thin on the ground, but his presence increases the likelihood of the break staying clear to win.

So, swings and roundabouts.

Today's route profile was up and down all day. A large(ish) climb peaked with thirty-odd kilometres to go leaving a descent much of the way to the finish in Carcassonne. The main contenders were happy to let de Gendt and his merry band have their day, and whoever got over that final climb up the front was in the hat for a stage win.

Rafa Majka – a pure climber – was first to crest the summit, but the group that followed included Magnus Cort Neilsen; a Danish sprinter who, it turns out, can climb a bit too. Once Majka was reeled back, Neilsen was *the* guy from a group of eight with a fast finish.

The eight worked together and made like a turbine: rotating with, against, and leaning into that hairdryer of a wind until Bauke Mollema, Jon Izaguirre, and Neilsen were left clear in a final group of three.

If, by any chance, you're busy making your own list of the next generation of winning pro cyclists twenty-five-year-old Magnus Cort Neilsen should probably be on it. Somewhere near Jasper Stuyven I would've thought. Though, I might add, if you're making such a list and you're *not* a TV commentator (and therefore in need of the aide memoir) you probably need to have a look at your life choices.

Get a hobby.

Make some friends.

And even if you *were* a TV commentator you wouldn't have needed those notes today. There was little nuance involved or knowledge required. A suspenseful three-up cat and mouse did not ensue.

Our friend Magnus sat on the front and waited serenely for either Mollema or Izaguirre to launch their "sprint". Once they did – I forget which of them, it scarcely matters – *he* launched *his*, and the race was over. The summit of the final climb – the Pic de Nore, thirty kilometres further back – was his finishing line.

Mollema and Izaguirre are fine riders, better than Neilsen in other areas, but cycling is cycling. Neilsen has the bigger sprint, and no amount of tactical manoeuvring was going to change that.

At the conclusion TV's Ned Boulting made the rather bold, if slightly inelegant claim that Neilsen was potentially a mini, though much taller, Peter Sagan. I'll put it on my list, against Magnus Cort Neilsen, in the "comments" column.

stages 16-18: THE PYRENEES

stage 16

Today, on stage sixteen, the riders had a new enemy to contend with. It combined with our old foe, the wind, and a whole peloton's worth of the world's finest bike riders were brought not only to a halt, but to *literal* tears. We're talking the likes of Froome, Thomas, and Sagan, crying like babies at the roadside.

I'm referring – and I'm somewhat surprised about it - to pepper spray.

That a group of French farmers flung some hay bales across the road and brought the race to a halt after around thirty kilometres is not news; French farmers have a history of protest, and few of us would begrudge them their traditional moment of belligerence. The Tour is not the Tour without one such incident.

What *is* news is that the French police cracked open the pepper spray with the eagerness of a British reveller going at the Friday night Prosecco.

Unfortunately, they (the French police, not the British revellers) didn't stop to consider the wind direction which was, as became apparent, peloton bound. Hence Sagan and co. found themselves in the firing (spraying?) line.

In the interests of fair and balanced reporting we have to fully consider the motives of the police. We are making the assumption that the targets of the pepper spray were the farmers rather than the cyclists. Rumours that it was a heavy-handed police response to those white shorts adorning the haunches of the Fortuneo-Samsic team are, at this point, unconfirmed.

French climbing hero Warren Barguil and his pals are certainly committing a fashion crime, of that there's no doubt, but I refuse to believe French authorities have chosen pepper spray as a proportionate response.

Thankfully, with plenty of soothing words and washing of eyes, the flow of tears was stemmed and the stage rambled on through the countryside, and over the mountains, towards Bagneres-de-Luchon. The overall General Classification contenders were content to conserve energy. The action happened up front, and largely on the slopes – both up and down – of the final climb: The Col du Portillon.

The pull to the summit was a study in contrasts. There was Robert Gesink, swaying and swinging like a limp sunflower in the Pyrenean wind. Not pretty. There was Adam Yates, tiny, a pure climber, and on the escape off the front of the race. And there was Julian Alaphilippe: French, polka dotted, and charismatic.

Dancing on the pedals like Contador. Goatee bearded like Pantani. Gurning like Voeckler for the cameras. You've got a favourite cyclist? He's got them covered. His was the climb of a man in a purple patch; confident in his legs and picking his moments.

Yates summitted first, Alaphilippe shortly after, and the ten-kilometre downhill chase began - and there's a drama about a descent into a Pyrenean town that makes the hairs stand up on the back of the neck[37].

Alaphilippe, you may be aware, descends like the devil. At the plunge of the descent Yates would've known very well that the Frenchman was on his tail. Often hindsight is the whimsical post-stage writer's best friend, but something was surely going to happen. It was in the air. I could feel it in real time in my twitching left leg and white-knuckle grip on the settee.

Sure enough Yates lost a front wheel on a hairpin, Alaphilippe caught him and swept past but then wonderfully, empathetically,

---

[37]*Remember Thor Hushovd, descending like a runaway train into Lourdes, in 2011? If you don't, then do yourself a favour and YouTube it.*

tried to wait for him. More like a human being than a sportsman, sensing the unfairness of Yates's tumble.

Alas, we can assume Alaphilippe's team boss stepped in sharpish with a screeching whaddya-think-ya-doin' on the team radio; message received and understood, and he burst off down the road to capitalise on his opponent's misfortune for a joyous win. All smiles, salutes, and disbelieving shakes of the head.

A proper French victory.

The polka dots, come Paris, will surely be his. Deservedly so.

stage 17

The riders lined up for the start; as advertised, this was not than the usual, tried and tested mass roll-out. No. We had "innovation" in the form of a staggered Formula 1style grid.

Kind-of.

If you squinted and pretended it made any sense.

With race leader Thomas in P1, the main contenders laid out in rows behind, and the remainder of the race penned in behind extra, additional start lines. For this glorified photo-op (for that is what it was) the riders had brought their A-game of casually deliberate. Sitting astride top-tubes, wrists a-rest on bars, and impassive.

Whoever came up with this idea had perhaps never seen a bike race. Or heard of cycling. It was a decision, as David Millar put it, made over a long lunch.

The tension rose. The start lights went out, and...GO!

The riders clipped in slowly, deliberately, and rolled lazily away. The pack of the peloton shuffled. Team-mates found team-mates and assumed a position, and we had a fully-formed standard-issue peloton ready to race. We hadn't *really* expected them to pelt away from the line, jockeying for position like Hamilton and Vettel heading for the first corner, had we?

Mild amusement fluttered all around and the "B" of the bang stage start experiment was done and dusted. An oddity of the 2018 Tour de France.

We'll take the positives though; the stage was underway, and that's a pretty crucial component of any bike race. And as stages go it was short (sixty-five kilometres) and sharp, with three big climbs, culminating in the – and there's really no other description for it - sustained brutality of the Col du Portet.

The first climb thinned the peloton like a fine-toothed comb raking the delicate hair-do of an ageing club singer. Sprinters and tired riders were shed, and a smattering of here-and-there groups were established up the road. In the thick of the thinning – naturellement – was our polka-dotted hero Julian Alaphilippe.

The second climb saw further developments, with Sky bossing the front until Romain Bardet put his young upstart of a teammate Pierre Latour to work on the approach to the summit. Bardet, you see, is a skilled and daring descender, and he was setting something up.

No doubt.

It's coming.

Any minute now...here we go.

Alas no. The patented Bardet swallow dive didn't arrive. He couldn't, or wouldn't. Latour, turned inside out, for nothing.

At the base of the *final* climb Alaphilippe, tired at last, gave the classic throat-slit gesture for the cameras. Done. So Nairo Quintana was the man to make a move. He borrowed the wheels of teammates Soler, and Valverde, before launching clear, alone, with a lead that he'd never lose Reminding us all in fine style just what a relentless mountain goat of a cyclist he is for a percentage of time which decreases from season to season.

Dan Martin, gasping and chasing like a demented wind instrument, got close, while behind, a grinding attrition was underway. It was exciting in the same way as growing your own vegetables is exciting; slow-motion, time-lapse attacks from Roglic, Froome and Dumoulin, that promised to produce something edible, eventually.

The unfortunate Bardet, struggling now, was cooked. Stir-fried. Sautéed. His Tour all but gone.

Froome, on the other hand, was showing imperious control. Back and forth through the group, sizing things up, a word for Geraint Thomas here, a quick chat on the radio there. Until, gently at first, and then unmistakeably, he began to lose wheels. The yo-yoing now looking less like a plan and more like a tired cyclist scratching and scrabbling for position. One trademark time-trial attack from Dumoulin and Froome was beaten.

The Sky man, in need of assistance, called back Egan Bernal the Colombian wonderkid, but to no avail. The combined weight of a Tour de France, a Giro d'Italia, and a Vuelta Espana finally caught up with him. He needs another of his near miracles to come back from this.

At the run in to the finish Geraint Thomas, capping a consummate Yellow Jersey ride, nipped a handful of seconds from Roglic and Dumoulin and settled the Sky leadership debate for another day. At the finish, as at the start, casual, yet definitely deliberate.

stage 18

A slow day on Le Tour. A lull. Tomorrow is a big day of Pyrenean punishment and legs are being saved. For the armchair fan these are the days where there's not much to see. Snacks are eaten. Time is passed. The mind wanders. Strange thoughts drift in and out.

Like, how does Chris Boardman manage to be Greater Manchester's Commissioner for Walking and Cycling, *and* a lynchpin of the ITV cycling coverage, *and* the figurehead of his own bike brand, *and* the father to six children?

It just sounds so busy.

Are we sure there's only one of him?

Is it possible...surely not...that he's cloned himself!? After all, the Venn diagram of pro cycling and progressive politics has very little overlap; if he was appearing in front of a government select committee whilst simultaneously recording pithy TV links with Ned Boulting would anyone *really* notice?

Maybe the famous "Dolly the sheep"[38] experiment all those years ago was just a way of testing the technology before it was rolled out on Boardman, in the service of his quest to be the busiest man in Western Europe.

Also, what the hell is a Commissioner for Walking and Cycling? Did he just stroll into Manchester Town Hall one day and say:

"Now listen here...I'm Chris Boardman and I've just invented a new job for myself. When do I start?"

Like I say – strange thoughts.

Anyway...

---

[38]*Dolly the sheep, for those of you who don't remember, was the first mammal ever to be cloned, back in 1996. At the time it felt like the end of the world was nigh. Here, in 2018, it still does. Though for different reasons. The idea that a cloned sheep might be the cause seems quaint, to say the least.*

For those of you still reading, and interested in what happened *today*, stage eighteen of Le Tour, it may have looked like nothing much to us, but to Arnaud Demare it was his very reason for being.

As a variety of sprinters have suffered and said goodbye through the mountains of this race Demare has very visibly hung on by the skin of his gritted French teeth. He's done that for two reasons: to try and win today, on the flat-out sprint to Pau, and again on the Champs Elysees on Sunday. And in a slightly ragged end-of-term sprint, thinned out by tired legs and those multiple withdrawals, Demare's team got organised and delivered him.

He finished the job beautifully.

As for our race leader Geraint Thomas I imagine he'll have had a few strange thoughts of his own today. Largely about tomorrow. A nervous paranoia perhaps kicking in. Wondering what tricks Dumoulin, Roglic, Kruijswijk and Bardet might have up their sleeves.

A metaphorical target drawn across his back, and the cream of pro cycling loading arrows into quivers.

Sleep well Geraint.

stages 19-20: A NEAR-RELIGIOUS EXPERIENCE

stage 19

To avoid the lapse into terrible cliché as the race rolled out from the holy town of Lourdes today was really the only ambition of the collective cycling media.

We could've mused on Romain Bardet and his need for divine intervention to haul him back into the race. We could've described the crowds on the slopes of the Col du Tourmalet parting like the red sea for Julian Alaphilippe, Tour director Christophe Prudhomme playing the role of Moses.

But actually, Lourdes, drowning in a sea of fake plastic religiosity, is a God-awful place. The riders did the right thing in getting out of town ASAP. No-one, least of all a Tour contending pro cyclist, needs a two-foot plastic Jesus table lamp. And for spiritual, other-worldly intervention, the Pyrenean Mountains are more than capable of delivering.

When all is quiet and the peloton are rolling along, conditions are benign. The riders chatting, eating, teasing Vincenzo Nibali about his refusal to smile about anything, ever, and thinking up new nicknames for Julian Alaphilippe (Begbie, from Trainspotting?). Skies are blue and the air is still.

The tension, today, didn't arrive until the riders reached the Col d'Aubisque. The final mountain of the Tour and the last chance for Dumoulin and Roglic to crack race-leader Geraint Thomas.

And as the end-game unfolded the Pyrenees did what the Pyrenees does.

The cloud began to roil and boil in the background. Great cavernous drops at the edges of our TV screens filled with weather, as visibility closed in and a claustrophobic set-piece began. The scenery green-screened away, distance and perspective removed, focus drawn to the cyclists.

The Pyrenean drama-o-meter was turned up to ten.

As that group of main contenders and their supporting cast – Thomas, Bernal and Froome, Roglic and Kruijswik, Dumoulin and those great, long, flamingo legs – swooped over the summit for the plummet to the finish, the fog was thick.

The assumption that a Tarmac covered corner or straight lay somewhere amongst the weather was enough for the riders to assume an aero tuck and keep fingers away from brake levers. Not looking for the apex but pointing a front wheel at the thickest patch of fog and following the wheel in front.

And the wheel in front was former ski-jumper Primoz Roglic.

It was hard to tell through the gloom but I'm pretty sure at one point, as he lay tucked across his top-tube, those arms v-shaped out behind him, instinctively, in the search for speed. Either way he slipped off into the lead, won the stage, and unceremoniously elbowed Chris Froome out of the podium positions.

It was a blistering win.

"Future Grand Tour winner," we all muttered, as if accessing some mysterious well of cycling wisdom (rather than stating the bleeding obvious).

Behind Roglic, the others finished as a chasing group to leave Geraint Thomas rock-solid in yellow. The Pyrenees had done their best but the group ambush in the fog never materialised for the simple reason that Geraint Thomas is, as he has been all race, just too strong.

A non-event was exactly what he needed, and he made sure of it in the way that Grand Tour winning cyclists sometimes have to. Because he's already done the exciting bit, and a Grand Tour winning cyclist is now very nearly what he is.

As Geraint Thomas crossed the finish line, having completed the stage twenty time trial and final competitive stage of the Tour de France of 2018, he delivered the classic primal-roar-look-to-the-skies-double-fist-pump of the pro sportsman.

That was the release.

The acknowledgement of the achievement.

Photogenic and heroic.

Then he was collared by a press man and asked a question. He opened his mouth and the lip trembled. He hid his face beneath team issue baseball cap (should be a casquette[39], really, but whatever...) and sobbed, squeezing out a manly "aww jeez...I don't know what's wrong with me," and then he sobbed a bit more.

Because he's a man in a man's world he'd rather not be crying for all to see, and I can feel the vibes radiating from my wife, sitting beside me, watching this heroic Welshman crying on TV.

She's thinking "there's nothing *wrong* with you, you're feeling an emotion you idiot."

---

[39] *The casquette, the classic cotton-peaked cycling cap, has fallen out of use out on the road since the advent of compulsory helmets. Leaving the sport safer, but uglier. It's a shame, but the protective qualities of cotton are less than that of polycarbonate. It's been proved. I feel like some kind of graphene casquette might be the future, though my technical knowledge of graphene is tenuous, at best.*

And she's right, of course. And then I felt her elaborate on her thoughts (still internally; she didn't say a word but we've been married a long time and I can read her like a (self-help) book). Her facial expression and general body language went on to say:

"You're experiencing big feelings Geraint...the joy you feel is too big to hold inside...with the tears you're letting it all out."

And I know what you're thinking. You're thinking that's quite specific body language. But my wife, you see, is a dedicated and committed childcare professional. She reads all the books and knows all the words. This kind of language is common currency in our house.

Though I should clarify she loves the man as much as the rest of us. How can you not? He's the everyman. The antidote to the arch complexities of Sir Bradley and the bullet-proof polish of Froome. He was never going to win the Tour because he's too normal. He was destined to be the ultra-respected unfailingly loyal team man.

In the end, perhaps he's the only guy who could snatch the Yellow Jersey ruthlessly from the back of his team leader with a smile, and a joke, and end the race as bigger mates than they started it.

Which leaves me with only the small task of quoting page seven, paragraph five, of the big book o' cycling clichés:

"Barring mishap on the traditional ceremonial stage into Paris..." Geraint Thomas is the winner of the 2018 Tour de France.

Big feelings indeed.

stage 21

"See how uncomfortable he looks, drinking champagne on the bike and taking the applause of the crowd," said the Welsh man on the radio. "It really shows you how normal he is. He's a man of the people."

It's a nice theory.

I couldn't help noticing *all* the Sky riders looked equally awkward and unimpressed by the traditional slurp of fizz from a plastic glass on the roll towards Paris. Which leads me to the only sensible conclusion.

The French people, as we know, are not universally enamoured with Team Sky and their relentless winning. It's seems clear to me that, on behalf of the citizenry, and in order to claim the last laugh, the Champagne was not, in fact, Champagne.

Before you jump to your own conclusions, I'm not for a moment suggesting it was anything sinister. No. I'm simply proposing that some generic French race organiser popped the vintage Champagne back in the cellar and instead poured several glasses of the kind of rough Pinot Grigio usually served warm in a Wetherspoons pub on a Wednesday night.

Luke Rowe certainly gave the confused, slightly alarmed face that I give when I drink the cheap stuff. It's a face that says: "Yuck, errrmmm, yeah...that's enough for me thanks."

It was a cheap shot, on an otherwise classy final day. Thomas negotiated it in the same calm, uneventful way he's negotiated the previous twenty.

Luke Rowe took to the front of the peloton with around ninety kilometres to go and upped the pace a bit; the sociable dawdle had begun to resemble a family bimble to the ice cream shop and Rowe was getting bored.

"Right lads," he seemed to be saying, "enough of this - pop yourselves onto my back wheel and I'll have you in Paris before you can say domestique-deluxe."

Which indeed they were, leaving the Tour de France to deliver its final peacock's tail of time-honoured clichés for another year: Breakaways came and went; riders punctured and panicked on the city streets; the TV director showed off his long, lingering, side-on shots of the riders bouncing and juddering over the cobbles; and that swooping shot of the obelisk at the Place de la Concorde filled our screens lap by lap.

All was present and correct.

And in the final knockings of the final stage, the riders grinning and demob happy, Alexander Kristoff won the sprint and Geraint Thomas won the Tour de France: a fact that was simultaneously predicted by no-one and yet, strangely, came as no surprise.

The most normal thing in the world.

Geraint Thomas, Tour de France winner 2018.

And with his speech – in which he committed to thanking his teammates by reeling off their names, got stuck after about four, had a bit of help from his main rival Tom Dumoulin to reach seven, and then remembered *he* was one of the eight – he managed to end the day even more endearingly than he started it.

The Welsh man on the radio was right; he's a man of the people.

tour de france 2018 final standings

1st Geraint THOMAS (WAL: Team Sky)

2nd Tom DUMOULIN (NED: Team Sunweb) +1'51"

3rd Chris FROOME (GBR: Team Sky) +2'24"

Points: Peter SAGAN (SVK: Bora-Hansgrohe)

King of the Mountains: Julian ALAPHILIPPE (FRA: Quick-Step Floors)

Young Rider: Pierre LATOUR (FRA: AG2R La Mondiale)

Combativity: Dan Martin (IRL: UAE Team Emirates)

Team: Movistar

Vuelta a Espana

Until fairly recently the Vuelta Espana was something of an afterthought. A relaxed affair. Not the frantic early-season frenzy of the Giro, nor the be-all-and-end-all of the Tour. Taking place in September, for many it was a race too far.

Charley Wegelius, a former pro who rode the Vuelta four times during the noughties, wrote about the race in his excellent autobiography, 'Domestique'. He likened the peloton to the crew of a pirate ship; it's end-of-term slot on the race calendar offering up a mix of riders who either don't want to be there or are desperate to perform. A ragtag band of mercenaries and desperados.

I don't think the peloton ever went *full* pirate – going rogue to loot and pillage the length of Spain, guzzling rum and singing shanties – but I can't *completely* rule it out. The noughties were a weird time in pro cycling.

Times have changed.

The Vuelta is now a prestigious and sought-after Grand Tour, but it's still, as it's always been, largely about the mountains. They are steep, and numerous, and tackled beneath the relentless Spanish sun. Much of the rest of the terrain, particularly the interior of the country, is sparse and dusty and resembles (in fact, in some cases, literally *is*) the backdrop for one of Sergio Leone's spaghetti westerns.

All of which is bookended by the lush green of the north, and the seaside of the south.

For the average cycling fan, never mind the average pro cyclist, it's a test of endurance. To commit to watching an entire three-week race requires enthusiasm and fortitude, and by September this is in short supply. We feel we've probably seen every variable in pro cycling over the previous nine months and have no real desire to see them again. We've got spectator fatigue.

In anticipation of this, and in an attempt to draw an audience, the organisers tend to chuck an entire kitchen sink's worth of gimmickery and talking point into the mix. In recent years we've had a time-trail (literally) on the beach, a selection of loops in and around tourist attractions, and always – always – a hitherto unridden climb that is *definitely* the hardest climb in Spain.

Since that other one last year.

As a fan, the trick with the Vuelta is to immerse yourself. It's like a slow burning box set of US drama. Nothing of any consequence happens for the first four or five episodes then episode six grabs you by the lapels and pins you, eyeballs first, transfixed, to your TV screen.

Give it a chance: it rarely disappoints.

The 2018 edition took in just shy of three-thousand-three-hundred kilometres. It began with a whistle-stop of trashy tourist towns before embarking on a dedicated avoidance of anything resembling flat Tarmac.

For twenty-one stages the road went up, and down, and then usually up again. Breakaways stayed clear, sprinters – admittedly thin on the ground - fought over scraps, and the contenders for the General Classification displayed a near pathological commitment to scaling mountains at pace.

As for looting and pillaging, police reports confirm it was kept to a minimum.

stages 1-2: THE COSTA DEL SOL

stage 1

With the seaside scenery of the Costa del Sol providing our backdrop for the short, blur of a stage one time-trial, the cliché generator in my brain is at full pelt. My senses are filling in the gaps.

I can smell a heady mix of sea salt and sun cream. I can taste calamari – battered, doused in lemon, and dredged through garlic aioli. I'm bloated with cheap lager and busily plotting against the Germans and their crack team of sunbed baggers.

I am British, you see, and the Costa del Sol comes with baggage.

One can only hope the riders turned down the Jaeger-bombs and left the club last night at a reasonable hour, alone, to settle down for a full eight hours. Avoiding the temptation, of course, to rise late and demolish the all-you-can-eat gut-buster breakfast at the nearest English caff.

In my experience, admittedly twenty years ago, a place like Malaga is teeming with the potential to compromise athletic performance.

Thankfully, most of the riders appeared at the start line bright eyed, bushy tailed, and unsullied by the underbelly of Spanish resort life.

Although with Vincenzo Nibali it was hard to tell whether his eyes were bright or not. He took the start ramp resplendent in a gold aero helmet featuring a swish, curved, reflective visor, as if in homage to Star Wars' Boba Fett. All sealed in and mysterious, like a highly competitive Lycra encased bounty hunter.

Had my fifteen-year-old self seen that helmet he'd have thought it the coolest thing in the world, added it to his Christmas list, and mimicked Vincenzo Nibali for the next five years in an attempt to make it as a pro cyclist. Of course, a fundamental lack of talent would've caught up with him eventually, no matter how cool the helmet.

Co-incidentally, the sealed in and mysterious look matches the Sicilians public image beautifully – Nibali not being a man for whom the words laid-back, relaxed, or indeed friendly are often used.

As my mind wandered, busily passing the time pretending to enjoy watching a time-trial, Nibali's Boba Fett helmet had me musing on the fun that could be had by kicking off a Grand Tour with a Star Wars theme. You would think La Vuelta, with its penchant for wacky innovation, would be all over this.

Back in 2015, for example, the opening team time trial rolled into Marbella along the sea-front using wooden ramps, a raised bridge section, and a lengthy stretch of rubber matting along the beach. A Star Wars theme is surely only a pedal stroke away from this contrived lunacy?

Unfortunately, my imagination then lingered a little too long on the idea of Victor Campenaerts folded into his TT position clad only in skimpy Leia bikini and I had to go and have a little sit down and a stern word with myself. I've since gone cool on the idea.

Our early leader today was Team Sky's Dylan van Baarle. He assumed that most awkward of TT positions (and it's a discipline that knows an awkward position when a crack team of aerodynamicists see one) in the hot seat, in front of a TV screen at the finish line, and forced to produce a visual reaction for the cameras each time of anyone of any significance posted a time.

Worryingly, he appeared to be entirely alone; in solitary confinement, held against his will, and cut off from any human contact. Slightly sinister. Was this a hostage situation, I wondered, a kidnap carried out in plain sight?

More likely the race organisers were taking no chances. In high season the streets of Malaga, awash with crowds of British tourists sharing drinks, bodily fluids, and who knows what else, are no place for a highly-tuned athlete. This was not a staging area in the post-ride TV tent but a quarantine facility. Perhaps the same reasoning lay behind the Nibali helmet; not so much sealed-in and mysterious as a proportionate response to a public health issue.

The relief that swept across van Baarle's face as Nelson Oliveira bettered his time and took his place was palpable. Oliveira was then beaten by Michal Kwiatkowski, who in turn negotiated his release at the expense of our first race leader and wearer of the Red Jersey Rohan Dennis; the Aussie adding to his growing collection of Grand Tour leading jerseys.

And yes, I agree: it would've been more entertaining had he managed this dressed as an Ewok.

stage 2

There are many things about Alejandro Valverde that might be described as "implausible". There's that near-bald pate masquerading as a head of hair, the consistently high quality of the gunslinger stubble, and the, ahem...*history*.

You know the one.

It's the same history that many pro cyclists from the early noughties have to reckon with. Involving murky behaviour and dodgy doctors. Only in Valverde's case it's largely un-acknowledged.

And there's one more implausible; those thirty-eight years of age. Not in itself an uncommon age for a Spanish human. The unusual bit is the concurrent winning of bike races. Even as I write this I feel a single eyebrow straining to raise itself involuntarily. Because people don't usually win prestigious bike races at thirty-eight.

He has the guile and craft of a wily old pro – a brutal pragmatism combined with a mastery of mind games – firmly attached to the body of a cyclist apparently in his prime. He demonstrated this today, yet again, in dispatching Michal Kwiatkowski into a second place that perhaps should rightfully have been his.

As Laurens De Plus, the obligatory late attacker from the Quick Step team, burst clear with a kilometre to go, the peloton watched and waited. Valverde, finally, could wait no more, and chased him down, helpfully towing along Kwiatkowski in the process. The Polish rider had set this up to a tee. His job was now to sit on the Spaniard's wheel and jump clear for the win.

Kwiatkowski did indeed jump, assuming Valverde had shot his bolt, and perhaps encouraged and cajoled to do so via some subtle and unseen piece of psychology from our man. But the Spaniard had another effort left. Implausibly so, you might say. *He* latched on to Kwiatkowski's wheel and gave it one final acceleration to take the win. An absolute masterclass.

Kwiatkowski got the runners up prize – the Red Jersey of overall race leader – while Valverde took the glory of the stage. At thirty-eight years of age, let's not forget. Implausible.

Can we get a check on that?

Does carbon-dating work with cyclists?

All of which brings us to our latest Richie Porte update; we are, after all, two days in to a Grand Tour, which means the likeable

Aussie has no doubt suffered some kind of terrible misfortune. Drum roll please...

On this occasion we are talking a humdrum but no less debilitating case of pre-race gastroenteritis. Today he found himself several minutes back in the company of stage one winner Rohan Dennis. A coordinated two-pronged double-team effort from Movistar and Sky, the teams of Valverde and Kwiatkowski, didn't help.

As the stage entered the final thirty kilometres they, in tandem, upped the pace, before nudging it slightly higher, and then accelerating away from any other rider not on tip-top form. Riders were shelled out the back like high speed peas into a crisp spring salad; we're talking Porte, Dennis, Adam Yates, Nibali, Sagan. Great bike riders, tough day on the bike.

The Vuelta Espana used to be known for a near-holiday camp atmosphere and some lovely relaxed racing. No more. Unless your idea of a holiday is physical pain and mental torment. Which for Valverde, if I've judged him correctly, I think it probably is.

stages 3-4: ARID LAND AND OLIVE GROVES

stage 3

Every year in this race, as we know, the sprinter's stages are full of hills. This leaves guys who, in the respectful words of David Millar on ITV commentary duty, are: "certainly not second-rate sprinters, just different sprinters."

Italian champ Elia Viviani, a man who is not afraid of an uphill gradient, was today's favourite. Matteo Trentin, a serial Vuelta stage winner last year, was in the mix. Nacer Bouhanni, the rider who boxes in his spare time[40], was looking for redemption and couldn't be discounted.

After a season of spats and squabbles, and recalled to the Cofidis Grand Tour squad, the reappearance of Bouhanni somewhere near

---

[40]*He sometimes also boxes in his professional time, too. Try clearing your diary for a day or two then Googling "Bouhanni fight," or "Bouhanni punch," or "Bouhanni controversy," and you'll get the idea*

the spotlight demanded that the fighting analogies were dusted off and wheeled out for a proper airing in the Andalusian sun.

But I can't help applying them to Peter Sagan instead. The world champ, nursing his way back to form and fitness after a bruising Tour de France, looked to be pulling the Muhammed Ali rope-a-dope in response to the heavy George Foreman fists of Viviani. The "Fear in Andalusia," perhaps? For much of the stage he was dangling towards the rear, visibly encroaching on Steve Cummings territory and looking benign.

Losing heavily on points.

Cummings, for the uninitiated, is the laid-back laconic Brit. He spends ninety-eight percent of a Grand Tour at the back of the peloton saving energy. The remaining two-percent will see him engaged in the most outrageous solo escapade through the mountains you've ever seen.

Some of the most goose-bump-inducing stage wins I've witnessed have come from Steve Cummings[41].

But I digress.

Fast forward to the trashy tourist town finish at Alhaurin de la Torre today and, with three kilometres to go, Sagan was in position.

Up off the canvas, Vaseline smeared all over his eyebrows, and gum shield firmly in place. Around seventh or eighth wheel, breathing

---

[41]*Stage fourteen of the 2015 Tour de France springs to mind, YouTube fans.*

calmly through his nose and doing an uncanny impression of a fully fit Peter Sagan pondering over exactly *how* to break the hearts of Bouhanni and Viviani.

Had they punched themselves out and left defences down for a sucker punch?

No. It seems an out of condition Sagan can still *look* like the king of the world but he was contending by force of personality and muscle memory. When Viviani accelerated, Sagan's head dropped and the game was up. He rolled in third. Giacomo Nizzolo finished second, with a punch-drunk Bouhanni fourth.

And the biggest surprise of the day was that, unless I'm looking in the wrong places for my cycling news (I'm looking on the Internet – I'm pretty sure that's still the best place?) Bouhanni, the one-man headline generator, produced no recognisable fall-out whatsoever.

No rumbles. No aftermath. No arguments. No headlines.

Nothing.

I already miss the old Bouhanni.

stage 4

A bumpy stage with a climb to finish, and the smart money was on another mano y mano between Valverde and Kwiatkowski.

Journalists, commentators, riders; all agreed this was the likely outcome.

Conditions were hot, sun was beating down, and the parched Spanish landscape was looking more wild-west than ever. One or two of the towns en route were, I swear, nothing more than clap-board frontages hiding movie-set saloons and whorehouses.

The peloton, sluggish, allowed a good break to go clear. Before long we knew our winner would come from one of eight. Valverde and Kwiatkowski not among them.

So that was that.

The number crunchers in modern cycling ensure that any rider who's a threat to overall race victory is never allowed to go clear like that. American Ben King, at just over four minutes, was the closest escapee to the leader's Red Jersey. And with less than twenty kilometres to go King – an unheralded twenty-nine-year-old pro – became the "virtual" leader of the Vuelta Espana.

For a moment that won't, in two-and-a-half-weeks' time, even attain the status of *footnote*, it was unreasonably exciting. Any cycling fan with a pulse thumping through their veins and a rudimentary understanding of the lure of an underdog was now willing him on. For the stage, and the overall lead of the Vuelta Espana, and it looked do-able.

An ambush, amongst the desert scrub of the south.

Alas, on the final climb circumstances conspired.

Down to two, King's companion was the Kazakh unknown Nikita Stalnov. We armchair fans had it all figured out. We'd done the deal for them. Stalnov does his work and helps King to the Red Jersey, and in return is gifted the stage win at the line. Standard. It's a classic deal. This stuff is woven into the sport like the working-together badge on the sleeve of a cub scout.

So they had their little chat. It didn't look to go well. The Kazakh, impenetrably, had his own ideas. For a while he took to riding alongside King.

Alongside!

There's two of them.

This makes no sense!

Either take turns, ride ahead at a pace of your choosing, or sit on King's wheel and have him tow you. Those are your three options from the "Big Book o' Cycling Tactics." Heavily corroborated by "Physics for Dummies" and "Oh-My-God-What-The-Hell-Are-You-Doing-Have-You-Ever-Ridden-A-Bike-Before!"

Alongside!?

Combined with a burst of energy from the main group back down the road this nonsense ensured the gap was cut and race leading Red Jersey ambitions went out the window almost as soon as they'd rapped on it and whispered: "Hey...whaddya reckon?"

Pleasingly, when the two leaders reached the end game King dispatched his wrong-headed nemesis with a burst of speed to take his first Grand Tour stage win. Air was punched. Cheers were heard.

All of which leaves me to briefly mention the other big winner of the day.

Remember the Giro d'Italia back in May? Miniature British cyclist Simon Yates was utterly dominating the race, dancing up the mountains of Italy like a goat on a promise. With ninety-percent of the race ridden, to suggest someone other than Yates were going to win would've seen you banished from the sport and forced to watch golf, in shame, for the rest of your days.

And then, on the day of Froome's miracle on the road to Bardonecchia, Yates's (sporting) world fell to pieces.

To say he cracked would be like saying Cristiano Ronaldo is reasonably comfortable with his looks. His self-destruction was utterly heart-breaking (again, perspective fans, in a sporting sense). I felt sure, mentally, he'd struggle to recover from that.

I heard rumours he'd grown a big beard and gone to live off-grid in a log cabin. Rumours that may have originated with me, admittedly, but rumours nonetheless.

And yet, while Ben King was trying to decipher Stalnov's tactics Yates had assumed that funny little upright climbing position of his and was calmly dispatching the best climbers in the race. Gaining time. Laying down a marker. Casually wearing the largest recorded pair of shades in the known world.

Again, air was punched.

This time, though, and with the outcome of the Giro d'Italia in mind, I might hang fire on the cheering.

stages 5-6: THE FEAR IN ANDALUCIA

If you were in the market for a breakaway stage win at a Grand Tour you'd pick the Vuelta Espana. It's an opportunist's race, and the most breakaway friendly of the three; the Giro being bat-shit crazy from start to finish, and le Tour being too big and too important for anyone to leave anything to chance.

And at the 2018 Vuelta this is how you would go about it:

Firstly, you'd wait for stage five. On roads that roll up, and down, and end with a lengthy descent to the coast for a ten kilometre drag race into the town of Roquetas de Mar. The sun, of course, will be baking hot. Tough days lie ahead. Motivation to chase a break might be minimal.

This would be the day.

Secondly, you'd engineer some decent companions to share the workload. Say, Bauke Mollema, for example – regular top-ten Grand

Tour rider and conveniently already out of overall contention and no threat in this race. And, hmm...how about BMC's powerhouse Italian and professional break maker Alessandro DeMarchi? Strong and combative. Long of limb and capacious of engine.

Finally, be in possession of a half-decent sprint and save enough in your legs to demolish the pair of them at the finish.

All of which was clearly in Simon Clarke's plan today – the EF Education First rider executed to the letter. And post-ride he sealed the deal by showing himself to be rather pleasingly human: slightly surprised to have won, happy to run through his list of self-doubts, and grinning like a five-year-old with a bag of Tangfastics.

There were parallels with yesterday's stage.

Until stage four Team Dimension Data hadn't managed to bag a World Tour win all season, and then Ben King delivered. Until late afternoon today EF Education First were in the same boat. Fashion wise, delivering all season in spades, in terms of wins, not so much.

As the three of them jockeyed through town they were so evenly matched it wasn't so much cat and mouse, as cat and cat and cat. At least that's how it appeared superficially.

But Clarke was riding like a sprinter. Peering over his shoulder, marking moves, clearly happy to wait for the gallop. He telegraphed his intentions, underlining the bits about being in possession of good legs and having a pedigree as a fast finisher, and won his stage.

Six years after the last one.

The parallels didn't end there.

Remember yesterday when I became unreasonably excited about the fleeting possibility of Ben King snatching the Red Jersey from the shoulders of Team Sky? Well, we were in that territory again, in the shape of Frenchman Rudy Molard – one of three pursuers behind the front three and the virtual Red Jersey for much of the day.

Across the finish line the cameras tailed Molard and we awaited a Team Sky led peloton. He supped casually from a can of drink, feigning nonchalance.

"Pfffshh...Red Jersey?..Whatevs..." his body language attempted to convey. What it *actually* conveyed was almost certainly post-watershed, such was the enormity of the moment.

And gloriously, romantically, he did indeed end the day as race leader, to the tune of forty-one seconds. Cue millions of pro cycling fans furiously ad-libbing to each other about Molard's strengths, weaknesses, and character traits, whilst frantically Googling young Rudy to ascertain his strengths, weaknesses, and character traits.

Monsieur Molard...your fifteen minutes of fame await.

Team Sky, clinically, confirmed they'd made the decision to let Kwiatkowski's Red Jersey go for now; usurping Molard's brave race-leading gambit and relegating him to a right-place-right-time chancer. The lack of urgency in their chase had already said as much. Shame. A lone rider *genuinely* holding off the might of Sky would've capped off a great story.

I can't help thinking the really classy response from Sky would've been to simply congratulate him for being so strong today, though I suppose then we'd have criticised them for being patronising in the face of the glaringly obvious.

Ah well. If you'd told me after stage five we'd have a French rider from the Francaise des Jeux team leading La Vuelta I'd have said:

"Wow, amazing! Thibaut Pinot is finally getting his shit together?"

None of us (be honest) saw Rudy Molard coming.

stage 6

The Spanish, as we know, are the kings of the siesta; that civilised little afternoon nap that helps them avoid the heat of the day and recharge the batteries. During the Vuelta Espana I also like to partake.

By absorbing as much of the culture of our southern European cousins as possible I am better positioned to convey the colour and flavour of this great race. Later each day, recharged by my sleep, you'll find me out in the field at the back of my house in full matador regalia, cape in hand, outwitting the local bulls. Then it's a quick shower, and a massive bowl of paella at 10.30 in the evening.

It's the most civilised three weeks of my otherwise dull north-of-England year.

As it happened stage six, today, was prime siesta territory. Never has a Vuelta stage looked more likely to end in a sprint finish. The three-man break was doomed like a pretty actress in a horror movie, and the whole race was guaranteed to come back together for a showdown between Viviani and co.

With thirty kilometres to go the catch was made, and I happily nodded off. I'd only stayed awake so long for the rare sight of Richie Porte taking part in a breakaway. The mirror-cracking black-cat-encountering Tasmanian is usually a contender, but being forty minutes down in the race he'd headed up the road for a glorified training ride.

I then slept on through the finish, and awoke in a state of confusion. I checked in with the conclusion to the stage online to be met with stories of panic, time gaps, echelons[42], and all manner of drama.

"How long have I been asleep?" I wondered. On reading Nacer Bouhanni had taken the stage win my sense of perspective started to unravel.

"What year are we in? Is this 2022? Have I been in a coma? Is the combative Frenchman now the dominant sprinter in pro cycling?"

---

[42]*Echelons form when a strong crosswind forces the riders to fan out across the road, seeking shelter to the side of the rider in front. The road is only so wide, and so those who can't find shelter are dropped. The bike race is blown to pieces.*

Disorientated, I wandered into the kitchen to find my wife thoughtfully preparing the paella and suggesting I use a proper stain remover to get the grass stains from my cape. Once fed and watered I began to piece together events.

The very moment I'd nodded off, a shoddily protected bollard in a Spanish town had scythed the peloton into groups. At the same time, a change of direction brought crosswinds in to play and those riders not in the front group were now as doomed as the incidental extras in the aforementioned movie.

Wilco Kelderman and Thibaut Pinot lost time. Much slapping of thighs and thumping of bars was evident as the chasers crossed the line. Frustration rippled through the group. Explanatory monologues detailing how the split was missed were being hastily composed for use in the team bus.

Upfront, meanwhile, Bouhanni had indeed outsprinted Elia Viviani. The big favourite for the day and his lead-out man got their timings a touch awry and the fist-happy Frenchman took advantage in style. His celebration as he crossed the line was, I believe, the perfect delivery of a textbook right cross.

Not only photogenic, but belatedly justifying my heavy use of boxing analogy on stage three.

To make amends for today I have resolved to adjust the timings of tomorrow's siesta to ensure I'm awake, and alert, at the key moments of the race. I will simply add the two hours on to my morning lie in, rise just before lunch, knock back a few tapas, and then tune in to the bike race until it reaches a conclusion.

Viva la Vuelta!

stages 7-8: HOT AND EMPTY

stage 7

Spain, it occurs to me after watching stage seven wend its way through a vast, parched nothingness, is an empty old place. Each time the peloton rattled through another white-walled and dusty village its population doubled, briefly. The roads today seemed to depart from nowhere, in the general direction of oblivion, taking the circuitous route via ho-hum.

Albeit a very dramatic expanse of ho-hum.

Perhaps the lack of humanity explains the alarming narrowness of much of the Tarmac. The roads seemed, in fact, to increase in narrowness as the stage progressed. It would've come as no surprise had the stage finale been located at the very moment when perspective crystallised at its point of singularity.

It seemed wise to back a skinny rider for the win.

Perhaps the narrow roads were designed with a mind to actually, literally, physically whittle down the field a bit as we head towards the end of week one. Right now, at the end of stage seven, we have our full complement of one-hundred-and-seventy-six riders in the race.

Although it was more to do with the dust and gravel at some pretty hairy moments that had riders slithering, sliding, falling off, and grumpily calling out the race organisers post stage. Dan Martin and Simon Yates – balanced, calm blokes – suggested in their interviews that the organisers might quite like a crash or two for the benefit of the viewers, because how else to explain the roads?

They may have a point.

But all I could think was how on earth can Simon Yates make earnest, serious comment wearing those shades? I mean, I like the guy, and I want him to win the race, but these highlights are going out pre-watershed. Children might be watching. If you haven't seen them I suggest you visit Google images using a widescreen monitor and have a look. They are a feat of engineering.

Chief victim of the slippery surface was Michal Kwiatkowski, former race leader, who slid off in the closing stages and never managed to re-join the main group.

In the final kilometres, and in amongst a tough climb, a sketchy descent, and some windy roads into an uphill drag at the town of Pozo

Alcón, it was indeed a skinny cyclist who won. Tony Gallopin (or "galloping Tony" as literally no-one, except me, ever seems to call him) jumped clear with one big, decisive effort with a couple of kilometres to go, to finish unchallenged.

At which point he vanished into that aforementioned singularity.

Presumably into an as yet unknowable fifth dimension to become the stage winner and, unless he can span the dimensions in reverse before tomorrow morning, the first abandonment of the race.

stage 8

The easy option would be to describe Alejandro Valverde as a "Marmite" cyclist. But that would be playing right into the hands of the marketing people at Unilever, who have us evoking their product every time we encounter a thing that provokes a response in people, one way or another.

Those clever bastards.

I won't play their game.

Instead, I will direct you towards the Cambridge Dictionary and their definition of a word which nestles quietly in the "C" section, ready and waiting to pepper our conversation with implications of intelligence:

Caveat*; noun. a warning to consider something before taking any more action.*

It's a word that I first noticed in the early noughties. It was a time when, as Tony Blair and George W Bush did their best to sell the Iraq war to the western world, every public utterance appeared to require a caveat. It was a form of linguistic gymnastics designed to absolve everyone involved of any blame at all times.

Now, I'm not for a moment comparing Valverde to Tony Blair - all the evidence suggests the Spaniard had little or no involvement in starting that war – but in the interests of balance I have to point out that neither was Tony Blair implicated in Operacion Puerto, the big doping scandal that hit pro cycling back in 2006.

Until such time as the Spanish courts release the mystery blood bags for re-analysis, Blair remains innocent until proven otherwise.

All of which is my rather roundabout way of saying that passing comment on Alejandro Valverde is complicated. Everything needs a caveat.

Take stage eight, today.

In fact, take the whole of his Vuelta thus far.

Wouldn't it be marvellous if we could just sing from the rooftops about this man and his performances? His relentless competitiveness. His longevity. His ability to break a knee cap at the age of thirty-seven (at the Tour de France of 2017) and recover, barely missing a pedal stroke, to win prolifically again in 2018.

But we can't, because our common sense flicks our ear and jabs us in the ribs and gives us *the look*. The fact that he's never offered meaningful public comment on his ban between 2010 and 2012 for doping offences means that we, the fans, haven't squared his *past* in our minds. How can we even begin to square his *present*?

Today, after chasing down a three-man break in sweltering thirty-eight-degree conditions the riders were faced with a tough uphill sprint finish in the town of Almaden. At the sharp end we had a clutch of sprinters-who-can-climb and climbers-who-can-sprint – a mixed bag. In the final hundred metres Peter Sagan burst clear, and when he does that, no-one catches him.

But in his wake Valverde was delivering another masterclass. The ageing Movistar man leapt from the chasing pack, snatched Sagan's wheel briefly, and then surged past for the win.

It was stunning. And breath-taking. But it was Valverde. Bursting past Sagan with a giant virtual asterisk suspended above his head. Cheers from some, raised eyebrows from others. An unbridled fist-pump followed by a caveat.

None of us any closer to knowing what to think.

stages 9-10: SALAMANCA

stage 9

For the past few days we've had stage nine flagged as the day when Rudy Molard will lose the Red Jersey. Despite being a strong climber, this mammoth day out through the mountains would prove too much for our surprise race leader. He would crack, and someone more famous would assume control of the race.

Being a romantic, I was desperate for Molard to "do a Voeckler" and keep the race lead[43]. The dismissive certainty of the pre-stage predictions was a bit too hard-nosed for my taste. Correct, but hard-

---

[43]*At the 2004 Tour de France Voeckler, a young, unheralded French pro, became a national hero by taking the Yellow Jersey and holding it, day after day, against all odds. He was eventually crushed, brutally, by an American chap called Lance.*

nosed. I would have preferred the pretence of: "he could do it, couldn't he…wearing the jersey is sure to spur him on…etc. etc."

Alas no.

On the final windswept climb to altitude at La Covatilla he lost contact. The moment his will was broken, five or six kilometres from the summit, it was over. Just like that. Because that's how it happens. He lost minutes.

The world of French cycling did, however, still have cause to celebrate. Entire towns gathered in squares, firework displays were hastily arranged, Bernard Hinault, I hear, held a gathering at his Breton farmhouse, delving into his wine cellar for a special vintage to mark the moment.

And that moment came just a couple of kilometres from the summit of La Covatilla as Michal Kwiatkowski gently lost contact with the main group of contenders, his legs whispering in Polish:

"To wystarczy."

That's enough.

And with that we had a huge mountain climb in a Grand Tour with no Team Sky riders anywhere near the front. None. And the champagne corks began to pop.

UCI[44] president David Lappartient was reported to have wept, briefly, tears of relief, before sitting down to pen a withering critique of Dave Brailsford and his Anglo-Saxon methods. Finally on the front foot, if only for one day.

It's fair to say that the offending climb – La Covatilla – was a brute. A great shoulder of earth, reaching high altitude, with a searing wind ready to cut down any foolhardy attackers. From the day's break our hero from stage four, Ben King, was out alone on the slopes, with Bauke Mollema in pursuit.

It came down to a simple question: Who can suffer most?

Ben King, as it happens. Two career Grand Tour stage wins and counting.

Among the contenders behind no one dared expose themselves to that wind and the race for overall victory was neutralised. Only in the closing kilometres did sniping attacks come. While the likes of Lopez, Kelderman and Quintana pushed for the finish Yates hovered behind, not attacking but maintaining and managing. Alejandro Valverde faltered, seconds further down the road.

Before he knew what had happened Simon Yates had done what he hadn't wanted to do. The new race leader, accidentally, by a single second.

---

[44] *Union Cycliste Internationale – the sport's occasionally pantomime-esque governing body.*

Post-stage, he was sheepish. His stated aim here at the Vuelta was to ride within himself. Let others worry about the jersey. Bide his time. Save his legs for later.

Imagine being so good that you can *accidentally* take the lead of a Grand Tour.

stage 10

Stage ten really was about as flat as the Vuelta Espana gets. Still, the organisers still couldn't resist chucking in a canyon from which the riders had to escape, up the climb of the Alto de Fermoselle, around thirty kilometres from the finish. For the sprinters it was a bit like an episode of one of Bear Grylls' ridiculous "survival" shows.

"Right, we're going to pack you off into this canyon with nothing but a bike, some energy gels, and the entire infrastructure of an international sporting event..."

Those who escaped the canyon without mishap or misfortune knew they had a chance, on the flat run-in, to win the race.

The sprinters at the Vuelta, of course, come prepared for a few climbs. The ones who need a pan-flat parcours along which to unfurl their mighty sprint don't bother turning up. Marcel Kittel, for example, six-foot-two and eighty-odd kilos, is not a fan of the race.

I'm not saying he would go "full Grylls" – trapped in that canyon, drinking his own urine and eating raw snake for supper – but he'd get dropped for sure. With no hope of contesting the sprint he'd wonder what the hell he was doing in Spain and where on earth his next bottle of German engineered Alpecin shampoo might be coming from.

On that crucial climb today Bora Hansgrohe set a blistering pace, clearly attempting to drop sprinters and enhance the chances of their man Sagan. The peloton stretched behind them, and then frayed a bit, and splintered slightly, a whiff of jeopardy in the air. But no more than a whiff.

By the summit (by which I mean the lip of the canyon, of course) the peloton was still sizeable, with all the big names present and correct. The climb not quite enough to precipitate a survival situation.

The only riders who missed the cut and remained abandoned were surely there by choice. Tired of the bike race and delighted by the change of scene and the opportunity to test their survival skills. Relishing the prospect of a refreshing glass of the good stuff to wash down their slices of raw Viper.

These unstable characters shall remain nameless.

Beyond that, the finale was indeed a simple affair.

Viviani's Quick Step team seized control of the front of the race, peeling off one by one in the final kilometres, to deliver their man. He won for the second time in the race without drama in a finishing town that was, in fact, no more than a village. By some estimations the smallest ever finishing town (village) on a Grand Tour, with a population of a mere one-thousand and some.

Presumably every last one of them out on the street watching Viviani's win.

As for that canyon, we can only assume the dropped cyclists are still there. Perhaps having banded together, for strength in numbers, they're in the process of developing a rudimentary form of canyon democracy and busily attempting to procreate and assure the future of their new tribe.

Either that or the team cars picked them up and whisked them off to the hotel for a massage and a flight home.

Maybe we'll never know.

stages 11-12: RUGGED GALICIAN TERRITORY

stage 11

There are days when you watch bike racing on the TV and it looks like a bit of a jolly. The riders freewheel across the countryside, swapping small talk and Mario Cipollini anecdotes, before rousing themselves for something resembling a sprint finish.

Post-stage they are whisked away for a rub down at the hotel, a near Michelin-starred meal courtesy of the team chef, and a couple of hours of screen time before the team boss reads them all a story and tucks them in for an early night.

It's not a bad little life.

Today gave us the other side of that cosy little coin. Wherever the TV director cast our gaze we were met with a rider grimacing, a bike being cursed, or a career choice being regretted.

It was, we knew from the off, a day for a breakaway. The road roller-coastered across the landscape of northern Spain. Every man and his Lycra-clad dog wanted to get in the break. The first two hours of racing were ridden – and forgive me for using the technical term here – balls out.

What we ended up with was an all-star cast in the break: the likes of Pinot, DeMarchi, Mollema, Roche, Haig, and Rolland, up the road and clear of the main field. For a while, the break also included the race leader as Thibaut Pinot, by dint of a three-minutes-and-some gap back to the peloton, became the "virtual" red jersey; virtual (rather than actual) leadership having proved something of a theme of this race.

On this occasion, it pleased me greatly; Pinot is a rider I can't help but love. A slightly flawed character, perhaps – in the context, of course, of being a world-class bike rider – but I do like a flawed character. They are forced to make up for those flaws with panache, and daring, and risk taking.

For a while Pinot had the look of a man about to "do a Froome." He rode clear of the break in search of an epic, race winning, career defining, social-media confounding solo win.

Unfortunately, Pinot was not sprinkled with whatever magic dust Froome discovered that day, earlier in the year, in Italy. His first move didn't succeed so he tried, tried, and tried again. Full marks for effort. And persistence. But it came to nought.

By the finish he had shed all the time gained and snatched a mere eleven seconds from race leader Simon Yates. In terms of a simple cost-benefit analysis not quite a roaring success. In terms of Pinot throwing his hat, his coat, and the contents of his sock drawer into the ring, a wonderfully doomed effort.

Who (apart from Dave B and the Team Sky boffins) wants clinical cost-benefit analyses anyway? Chapeau Thibaut!

While all this was going on BMC Racing were busy setting up their man Alessandro DeMarchi; not just a breakaway specialist, but a Vuelta Espana breakaway specialist. His win today the third such Vuelta stage win of his career. As he crossed the line, with a final grimace, he was too tired even to celebrate properly; not so much punching the air as waving a weary arm in its general direction.

In the post-race interviews he had the hollow-eyed look of a man who's been to a dark place and doesn't want to talk about it. I reckon he's earnt an extra bedtime story in the team hotel tonight.

stage 12

Spanish cyclist Jesus Herrada is no mug. Having said that, neither is he the second coming. He's somewhere in between, as most of us are.

He found himself in a breakaway today that was given a particularly long leash by the peloton. So long, in fact, that he was metaphorically sniffing around in next door's garden, rooting through their bins, and happily fouling the crazy paving. It was clear from as far out as fifty kilometres that we had our new race leader.

By the finish he had gently relieved Simon Yates of his red jersey to the tune of three minutes and some. In that horribly cynical, know-it-all way that modern humans have, the very moment he crossed the line to bag a surprise lead in this Vuelta Espana we said: "He won't win the race though...."

As if that were even the point.

Of course he won't win the race.

He is not in that elite category of riders who have the physiology and mentality to win a Grand Tour. You have to be a physical freak, at worst. At best you'll be some kind of messiah figure, able to tap into near miraculous powers. And as we've established Jesus Herrada is not the messiah...[45]

It's a funny old sport, is pro cycling.

Simon Yates accidentally took the race lead back on stage nine. Today, on stage twelve, he very deliberately lost it again. We understand why, of course: it frees him up to ride his own race, unencumbered by an absolute responsibility to defend the race lead, and allows him to ride in calculating, counter-attacking (race-winning?) style.

He also gets out of media duties post-stage.

---

[45] *I know what you're thinking, Monty Python fans. Now piss off!*

Jesus Herrada, on the other hand, gets his moment in the sun. The Vuelta gets a Spanish hero for a few days. Cofidis, sponsors of both the race and Herrada's team, get the required bang for their buck. All we need now is for someone in the Cofidis hospitality tent to turn all that bottled mineral water into Galician wine and we've got ourselves a fairy-tale.

stages 13-15: MOUNTAINS, AND MORE MOUNTAINS

stage 13

This morning, pre-stage, if you'd checked our respective Wikipedia pages you'd have noted that myself and Oscar Rodriguez, of the Euskadi Murias team, shared the same number of wins as a professional cyclist. Zero. Not one between us.

Today, on the vicious climb of La Camperona, the young Spaniard leapt ahead of me.

I just hope he's got a good lawyer, because he did this by employing Chris Froome's patented spinny-spinny thing; legs ablur, like a hamster on a well-oiled wheel. I understand the waggly-elbowed one can get quite litigious when people employ his methods without written permission. Thank goodness Rodriguez didn't also utilise Froome's weird aerodynamic frog-in-a-blender pedalling style on the descents.

On gradients that can only be accurately described as 'naughty,' our young hero for the day appeared to ride at a single pace from the bottom of the climb to the top. While silky Polish climber Rafal Majka and Belgian Dylan Teuns eyed each other up for the race win Rodriguez spun up from behind, spun level, and then spun away off into the distance.

For a guy who's never won a bike race before he sure seems to know how to win a bike race.

No one could have seen this one coming. He's a complete unknown. Apart from anything he has that generic Spanish name: Oscar Rodriguez. My conservative estimates suggest that as many as one in three male Spaniards (and one in five female) are called Oscar Rodriguez. It is *not* memorable, is what I'm saying.

Even Oscar's own mother, when asked to comment on her son's first pro victory, needed reminding who he was. Y'know the fella...Spanish looking...spinny-legs...god-awful black and flouro cycling jersey...you can't miss him.

That jersey; the only blot on an otherwise entertaining win. I understand that Euskadi Murias are a small team, on a small budget, but did they really have no choice but to kit their riders out from the local charity shop?

Behind our unlikely winner the battle for the General Classification took place in slow motion, on steep, steep slopes, Vuelta style. Towards the summit Nairo Quintana emerged a little further from his recent cocoon of lethargy to show himself to be approaching the kind of consistent form we haven't seen for a couple of years. Simon Yates, just behind him, was next best.

Post-race, Alejandro Valverde, Quintana's teammate, was asked whether today demonstrated that the Vuelta is to become a battle between Yates and Quintana.

"...and also one other," was Valverde's reply.

You're talking about yourself aren't you Alejandro? You cheeky little monkey.

stage 14

It's known an earworm; a song that lodges itself, on a loop, in your head. As a cyclist I regularly find myself accosted by this phenomenon. Sometimes it's a song I like. Often it isn't.

On stage fourteen today the riders reached the penultimate climb – the Alto de la Falla de Los Lobos – and the instant we glimpsed the lower slopes Eurosport's Carlton Kirby gave us all our internal soundtrack. "It was La Bamba wasn't it?" he said, "and the band was Los Lobos if I remember rightly..."

And all we heard was: "Para bailar la bamba, para bailar la bamba, se necesi una poca de gracia!"

Ok...what we *actually* heard was: "a la lalalalabamba...etc," because we hadn't had time to Google the lyrics before the earworm struck.

Either way, this tune was stuck in our head. Worse, having Googled it, I then discover that Los Lobos were an American band and La Bamba was a cover version of a Ritchie Valens track. Too much information. My knowledge of Los Lobos has just increased by several hundred percent, no doubt pushing something important out of my head to make space.

As happened to Homer Simpson: "Remember that time I learnt French and forgot how to drive?"

Anyway...the cycling.

We had another all-star cast in the break today, confidently leading the race in the direction of the final, steep, brutal climb of the Alto Les Praeres; four kilometres of leg-breaking Tarmac within an amphitheatre of fans. In that break were De Gendt, Woods, Roche, Kwiatkowski and Bookwalter.

Alas, with forty-odd kilometres to go its engine fell out. Thomas De Gendt, leading proceedings in his usual sledgehammer style, had a mechanical issue and dropped back. Michael Woods, perhaps the next strongest, crashed on one of those ever-tightening bends on the descent from Los Lobos.

Maybe the earworm distracted *him*, too.

After that, the rest battled on, but too much horsepower had been shed. Kwiatkowski reached the final climb alone and was swallowed up by the peloton. By this time the Red Jersey –our man Jesus Herrada- was minutes back, and we knew we'd have a new race leader.

The peloton was whittled down to the main contenders and we were treated to the sight of some of the finest cyclists on the planet having their legs slowly, and painfully, torn to shreds.

The climb hit twenty percent, crowds gathered, baying, but behaving. Carlton Kirby got excited, Sean Kelly less so, and Steven Kruijswijk threatened to ride away. Miguel Angel Lopez looked strong and made it his personal mission to annoy Quintana by diligently sucking his fellow Colombian's wheel.

Valverde lurked, as Valverde does.

All the supporting actors were in place and we waited for Simon Yates to make a move.

As he attacked in the final kilometre or so I carefully monitored his cadence. His legs were spinning quickly. Wasting no time I instinctively clicked on my generic music streaming service of choice, selected La Bamba by Los Lobos, and had my suspicions confirmed: Yates's legs were spinning at the exact RPM of that 1987 hit single.

La Bamba had propelled him away off the front to win the stage and politely remove the Red Jersey from the back of Herrada.

I half expect Spanish team Movistar to lodge an objection, but they'll get nowhere. Rightly or wrongly La Bamba is not currently on the banned list of the World Anti-Doping Authority.

Simon Yates, I expect, is just happy that Carlton Kirby's earworm of choice today wasn't one of Celine Dion's slow-tempo power ballads. For all kinds of reasons.

stage 15

For kilometre after kilometre of today's stage the baby-blue of the Astana team drove the pace on the front of the peloton. They flogged themselves. And buried themselves. And burnt their candles one by one. Miguel Angel Lopez was feeling perky. They were clearly setting him up for an attack on the Lagos de Covadonga, the set piece finishing climb of the day.

The Covadonga resembles a great staircase. It ascends in bursts of stiff gradient between sections which ease, or are flat, or occasionally very slightly downhill.

When people talk of the Covadonga – those who've ridden it, or know someone who's ridden it, or are just intrigued by the mildly amusing double-entendre laden name – they do so in hushed tones. It is a legend.

There's a church at the bottom of the climb: the Basílica de Santa María la Real de Covadonga. As the riders skirted past it I felt sure that Carlton Kirby, Eurosport commentator par excellance, would make reference to it. That the riders might be wise to offer a prayer before the climb. That divine intervention might be handy.

Instead, he fixated on the two massive bell-towers and we reached peak-Kirby. "Two great bell-towers there," he said, "the dingers on the donga you might say."

The metaphorical tumbleweed rolled through the house of every Eurosport viewer. Sean Kelly was silent. Kirby immediately apologised, realising that it was a faux-pas to reduce a venerated Catholic institution to the status of a knob-gag. He'd now made it impossible for any of us to refer to the 'ding-dong battle' that was about to ensue.

He'd shot our collective bolt too soon.

Nevertheless, with seven kilometres of painful climbing to go Lopez did indeed attack. To say his attack had been telegraphed would be a woefully outdated analogy. His competitors had been invited to join a WhatsApp group, accepted politely, and then immediately been sent that bike emoji with the puff of wind emoji behind it to make it look fast.

Shortly afterwards Thibaut Pinot attacked. This one had the element of surprise. Before you could say "social media blackout" Pinot was around the bend in the mountain mist and away. It looked like, and was, the stage winning move.

Thereafter, with Lopez and Pinot up the road, the rest of the contenders knocked lumps out of each other. Almost literally, at one point, as race leader Simon Yates, feeling he was doing all the hard work, waved his arms around angrily in the general direction of Valverde, Quintana, Kruijswijk and Mas. Further evidence that Yates is building a little reputation as a grumpy bugger, if I may say so.

Though in the end he calmly took third place, behind Pinot and Lopez, to extend his race lead ever so slightly. Whichever way you look at it the race dinged on the donga.

Which, if we're being brutally honest, makes no sense whatsoever.

stages 16-18: AUTONOMOUS UP NORTH

stage 16

As those of us watching this year's Vuelta are well aware, Simon Yates is managing to lead the race while simultaneously exploring his own personal sense of style.

I'm all for this: conservatively dressed identikit sports people are boring. But Yates is a work in progress; testing his own boundaries and fumbling for a personality like a teenage emo hankering for the shiny gloss of Taylor Swift.

This is particularly true above the neck.

Luckily, his time-trial position on the bike is stock still. This means I can stick a strip of gaffer tape on my TV screen right where his head is, relieving me of the need to look at those vast shades – constructed to the plans of an avant-garde architect by a team of structural engineers - encased in that elaborate aero helmet.

Which, I have to say, is quite an ornament. Camouflaged and shell-like, with great leaves hanging over his ears.

When it comes to style there's a fine line between daring and confident, and slightly alarming. It's the helmet/shades combo that a cutting-edge fashion designer would show on a Milanese catwalk before toning it down for the high streets; the cycling equivalent of a classic blue business suit with tin foil collars, a belt made of bacon, and cut-out bum-cheeks.

Bonkers.

I initially assumed he was taking on the TT in fancy dress for charity. Had Valverde rolled down the ramp as one half of a pantomime horse (with Quintana the other, of course), I would have happily applauded the fundraising efforts of *all* the main contenders and chucked a couple of euros in the bucket. But the helmet was a choice (albeit one tied up by a contractual obligation).

As for Rohan Dennis – pre-stage favourite turned dominant stage winner – there was no element of a frivolous costume. He and his bike just looked *fast.*

The sophisticated timing mechanisms said as much, but I'd have been equally happy to just trust my own eyes; gliding around the thirty-two kilometre course today he appeared smooth, slippy, and in union with his bike. Perfectly calibrated to sneak between the wind molecules.[46] He was the obvious winner.

Beyond Dennis the TT did what the TT does.

Within twelve minutes of completion no-one present can remember a single note-worthy detail other than the following facts: Quintana and Lopez finished several months behind the winner (my estimate...again, I'm happy to trust my own eyes on this).Steven Kruijswijk, the Angular Dutchman™, gave it the beans and scrambled his way up to a podium position overall. Valverde is second and Yates retains the Red Jersey.

It was equal parts important, necessary, and mundane.

Next year, when it's time-trial day at a Grand Tour, I'm going to host a TT party to liven things up. It'll be all back to mine where the drinks will flow (an easily digestible combination of carbohydrate and electrolytes, of course), the dress code will be "aero," and should anyone pop outside for a spot of fresh air they'll be followed by an estate car with their name written across the front.

Oh...and NO fancy dress.

stage 17

If you ever find yourself with exactly sixty minutes in which to explain the Vuelta Espana to a complete novice, the final hour of

---

[46]*What? Wind molecules. Ask a scientist.*

stage seventeen through the Basque country would be your weapon of choice.

One minute today's race was rolling through the lush green of this autonomous region, heading towards a final climb, friendly-looking Basque cycling fans cheering at the roadside. The next, from nowhere, it turned left up the side of a hill.

One look at the concrete 'road surface' told us that ten days ago there was no road there. There was a track, at best. Maybe a path. Goats and sheep gathered, roadside, in twos and threes to watch. Equal parts absorbed in the action and indignant at the race organisers for desecrating their well-trodden infrastructure.

The organisers of La Vuelta often spend the months pre-race tantalising the cycling press with mystical tales of the new, steep, and as yet unridden cols that await. I'm not convinced the upper slopes of the Balcon de Bizkaia ever fitted that description. This was a big hill with enough access to get a concrete mixer reasonably close – et voila! We have our big, bruising, set-piece unridden col.

As this strip of unwelcoming concrete unfurled itself we were led, a notch at a time, up the Vuelta-o-meter.

The road got steeper. Grinding along at a fourteen, then fifteen percent gradient, before launching into the mid-twenties – the mid-twenties! It was designed to offer an exciting spectacle, but no-one attacks on twenty-five percent Tarmac (or concrete, or anything).They're too busy maintaining forward momentum. And trying not to look silly on TV. It's a race, in slow motion.

On the steeper sections the fans form a cacophonous guard of honour, screaming encouragement and giving their favourites a little push (or a fondle, depending on their personal tastes and respect for societal norms). Basque flags fly, and Valverde the Spaniard lurks menacingly. The fans shake fists at their hero.

As the group of main contenders thins to the strongest, and bravest, whoever is in charge of atmospherics pulls the lever marked "fog" and a blanket of the stuff descends. Only Michael Woods, in EF Education First pink, is visible, and by this point he's the lone attacker out front. The bent, agonised figure of BMC's Dylan Theuns in sluggish pursuit.

Further back are Valverde, Yates, Mas, and brother Yates, pushing on their pedals in the assumption that the road does, indeed, continue in this general direction. Through the fog, it's hard to tell. Perhaps they're beyond caring. Were they to pedal off the edge at least the pain in their legs and lungs would stop, one way or another.

The four didn't so much hit the finish line as collapse across it, to be wheeled away by a helper for some kind words and a little lie down. Canadian Michael Woods, the winner, dedicated the win to his stillborn son, Hunter, lost two months ago.

Hearts melted and broke. Grown men cried. Emotion flowed.

And that, condensed into a single hour, is your Vuelta Espana. All of humanity can be found here.

stage 18

Lleida, our Catalonian finish town on stage eighteen, is an old place. *Really* old. Settlements are recorded here as far back as the bronze-age. In Roman times it was a flourishing city of some importance. Some to suggest it might pre-date even Alejandro Valverde's first win as a pro-cyclist.

For the riders today, however, I imagine any history and culture was lost on them.

On the way to Lleida they were preoccupied with the pain in their legs and the mountains of Andorra on the horizon. Post-stage they'll be flat-out in a hotel room, everything they need within their wingspan, trying to ignore the pain in their legs and the mountains of Andorra on the horizon. I've never ridden a Vuelta Espana – in fact I've been consistently overlooked for *all* the Grand Tours – but I'll hazard a guess that by stage eighteen, after racing a few thousand kilometres, the cultural significance of the start and finish towns has become a moot point.

At the start of the day the microphones were being shoved into the face of the likes of Viviani, Nizzolo and Sagan. The sprinters. The largely flat profile didn't so much promise a sprint as swear on its mother's life, no word of a lie, I'll leave my Rolex with you as insurance. Trust me. It's a sprint.

Which it was, kind of, but in a super-exciting edge-of-the-seat will-they-won't-they-the-breakaway-has-only-gone-and-hung-on-by-about-three-metres kind of way.

Out front all day, Sven Erik Bystrom and Jelle Wallays[47] had a lead of about fifteen seconds into the final kilometre. As Bystrom led, with Wallays glued to his wheel, the peloton wheeled into view down the lens of the finish line camera.

Usually, from here, comes heartbreak. The breakaway loses, the sprinter wins, and everyone forgets how close it was.

With a few hundred to go Sagan launched a die-with-your-boots-on sprint to bridge the gap. Meanwhile Wallays got the jump on Bystrom. A seething peloton's worth of fast finishers gasped and snorted just behind. For a brief moment all one hundred and seventy-odd riders were going to cross the line at exactly the same moment until Jelle Wallays, who wasn't having that, took it with Sagan three metres short.

The break hung on *and* we got our sprint finish. Two-for one. Total, high-pitched, sun-baked excitement.

You might even call it culturally significant.

---

[47]*Surely the most Belgian of all the names?*

stages 19-20: A CLINICAL TAX-HAVEN

stage 19

The simplicity of stage nineteen appealed to me. From the start in the previous day's finish town of Lleida the roads rolled uneventfully into Andorra, and to the foot of the climb of the Col de la Rabassa. From there the finish line sat seventeen kilometres up the road at a height of two thousand metres.

In profile, and for the benefit of any maths fans out there, an exponential curve; starting flat, and gradually rising, before peaking dramatically at the end.

Prior to the stage I detected a growing swell of support for Alejandro Valverde to win this Vuelta ahead of Simon Yates. With his wily race-craft he would pinch time here and there over the final two mountain stages. Perceived wisdom said so.

Wisdom compounded, perhaps, by memories of Yates' traumatic, utter collapse on stage nineteen of the Giro d'Italia earlier in the year.

Until he wins a Grand Tour he carries that particularly painful monkey on his back. With the extra weight, it's a good job he's a sixty-kilo skinny bloke.

But Yates had his own ideas.

In the final kilometres today he took matters into his own hands; the last thing he wants is a simian sidekick whispering in his ear, criticising his choice of helmet/shades combo and asking pointed questions about how his legs are feeling. He grasped that monkey, had a few choice words, and then dispatched it coldly and calmly.

He essentially murdered a monkey. A metaphorical monkey, but a monkey nonetheless. He may be about to earn the epithet of "Grand Tour Winner..." but it might come with a caveat of "...and ruthless monkey killer."

When he attacked, so far from the summit, he had Thibaut Pinot and Steven Kruijswijk to bridge across to; willing working companions both. Kruijswijk hunting time to leap back on to the podium, Pinot looking for a second stage win. The three of them pounded their way up the Rabassa, Pinot and Yates looking strong, with Kruijswijk hanging on a touch towards the top.

When Kruijswijk *did* crack the two rattled on to the summit where Pinot got his win and Yates took an almighty stride towards overall victory at this Vuelta. Alejandro Valverde, his challenger, was a minute-and-some further down the mountain and looking every bit his thirty-eight years; slightly laboured and wrestling with his bike.

Perceived wisdom in tatters.

The monkey, I choose to assume, received a respectful roadside burial from a caring fan.

stage 20

In Andorra, Simon Yates is on home turf. On the small handful of days each year when he's not trotting the globe being a top pro cyclist he calls this place home.

It's an odd place. The stunning mountainous beauty offset by the brutal infrastructure of a clinical tax haven. Nestled in the valleys are wide highways, modern comforts, and shrines to the Gods of capitalism. If you want shopping, Andorra might just be the place for you.

For the cyclist there are climbs a plenty to ride up, but not always suggestive of adventure, wilderness, or solitude. It's not a place to shoot a Rapha campaign, is what I'm saying. It seems to hit the spot for Yates though.

Six mountains in under a hundred kilometres today were designed to deliver fireworks. To be raced hard, in a flurry of attacks, for an edge-of-the-seat set piece Red Jersey showdown. Problem is, the cyclists are tired.

We sit, in front of our TV, a range of snacks and fancies in reach. We wonder whether we might walk to the pub later, whilst considering how much the local cab firm charges for half a mile, and we shout at the screen.

"Attack! Attaaaaaack! What the hell is Quintana doing? Valverde needs to attack...this is his only chance...etc. etc."

As if it hadn't occurred to Quintana or Valverde that to attack Yates, gain time, and relieve him of the Red Jersey, wouldn't be absolutely ideal. The perfect tactic. Certainly preferable to hanging on grimly, mountain after mountain, wringing out every watt of willpower in an attempt not to crack.

And on that final climb, with a handful of kilometres to go, Valverde did indeed crack. The TV cameras caught the moment. Something inside the veteran Spaniard snapped and we saw, instantly, that he'd been clinging to a precipice. His pace halved and the race rode alarmingly up the road and away from him.

It was a forlorn sight.

Quintana, team mate and co-leader, dropped back so they could both look forlorn. The Colombian slowed, and slowed again, before slowing enough for Valverde to sit on his wheel. The pair of them tumbling down the rankings.

Enric Mas and Miguel Angel Lopez, meanwhile, were up front duking it out for the stage. Simon Yates sat fifty metres behind them, calm, and in control. He'd reigned in his aggressive instincts in favour of a percentage game.

Never looking anything other than in complete control (at home, you might say), he crossed the line third to become Vuelta winner (in waiting...) and his head and shoulders slumped. In happy relief, I presume.

Cable taught muscles, both mental and physical, were given a moment of release. Tomorrow, in Madrid, he wins the race (barring accident).

(Touching wood.)

(Saluting magpies.)

(Executing the Mitchelton-Scott high alert black-cat-avoidance protocol.)

The stage winner was one Enric Mas, a Spanish rider I found no reason to mention until stage fifteen of this race, so under the radar was he. Mas is the protégé of old snake hips himself, Alberto Contador, and now officially the Next Big Thing™ in Spanish cycling. Picking his moment, as Valverde slid backwards, to claim that crown. Clawing his way up to a podium position overall.

A star is born.

It is rumoured that now Yates has achieved his Grand Tour goal he will relocate back to his home town of Bury, in Lancashire, to be closer to the famous Bury market and it's infamous black pudding[48].

---

[48]*It's pretty much made of pig's blood. Make your own mind up.*

Rumours started by me (as they so often are, fumbling for comedy amid the rigid strictures of pro cycling), admittedly; I find the idea of the man with the most multi-continental accent in pro sport living in a market town in the north of England unreasonably amusing.

The tax-rate might not be up to his usual standards but I'm sure he'd get some good, down to earth appreciation for his efforts:

"Now then lad...I see thi' winnin't bike race an' that...that were aw'reet that! Would ya mind signin' me black puddin'?"

stage 21: MADRID

I must admit, I was hoping for tears on the podium. Not "full Winslet" perhaps, but at the very least a quiver in the voice and a moistening of the eyes. This sort of behaviour is the fast track for any sportsperson into the hearts of the British public.

It wasn't to be.

Post-race, as mid-race, Simon Yates was as clinical as a Michelin starred tapas chef and as calculating as Dave Brailsford in a maths exam. That's not to say clinical and calculating can't be exciting. Each time the moment was right in this race he accelerated up the road like a rat up a drainpipe. Gone, without so much as a hasta la vista.

At times it was spine-tingling in its execution.

He backed this up with all manner of patron-esque behaviour; the "patron" being the boss of the race who calls the shots and ensures that etiquette is observed and standards of behaviour are maintained. Think Bernard Hinault punching a protester, or Mario Cipollini castigating riders for daring to race, at pace, while he was busy resting up during one of his many Giro d'Italia.

It's a title not so much bestowed upon a rider as assumed, with a swagger, and a what-you-gonna-do-'bout-it?

We saw Yates waving arms at rivals who he felt weren't sharing the load, yelling angrily at camera motorbikes who were getting a little too close to the action, and perfecting a general body language which said:

"I am not tired. You imagined it. Now *behave* yourself."

From the moment on stage nine when he accidentally took the race lead he's been *almost* apologetic in his dominance. Sorry-not-sorry. And here we are, ending 2018 with three *different* British riders in possession of the three Grand Tours: Chris Froome, Geraint Thomas, and now Simon Yates.

It's bonkers. It's implausible. Twenty years ago if I spotted a British rider just *pedalling along* in the peloton at the Tour de France I would literally wet myself. And now this.

It's almost too much.

The final stage of this year's Vuelta was the usual sleepy spin into Madrid followed by an eyeballs-out-five-abreast lunge for the line. King of the lungers was Elia Viviani who took his third stage win.

Way back at the Giro d'Italia you may remember me patronising Viviani, the single Grand Tour stage winner, and bemoaning the disrespect he endures. Now, by the end of the Vuelta, he's an eight-stage winner. Proof that he is definitively the greatest sprinter in the world.

Not including the Tour de France where he's about fifth.

As for Simon Yates, he doesn't strike me as the kind of guy to rest on his laurels. He will surely now attempt to win a ridiculous number of Grand Tours.

Having banished the ghost of Bardonecchia (and outwitted that pesky monkey) you wouldn't bet against him.

vuelta espana 2018 final standings

1st Simon YATES (GBR: Mitchelton-Scott)

2nd Enric MAS (SPA: Quick-Step Floors) +1'46"

3rd Miguel Angel LOPEZ (COL: Astana) +2'04"

Points: Alejandro VALVERDE (SPA: Movistar)

King of the Mountains: Thomas DE GENDT (BEL: Lotto-Soudal)

Young Rider: Enric MAS (SPA: Quick-Step Floors)

Combination: Simon YATES (GBR: Mitchelton-Scott)

Combativity: Bauke MOLLEMA (NED: Trek-Segafredo)

Team: Movistar

the warm down: A GREAT BRITISH GRAND-SLAM

Back in the early 1990's televised sport was hard to come by. Having had my fill of the beige buffet of crown green bowls and horse racing offered by the BBC, I found myself flicking over to Channel Four. Faced with a choice between Kabaddi and the Tour de France I picked the cycling, deciding that even for me - a contrary teenager with a snobbish disdain for anything mainstream - Kabaddi was a bit *too* niche.

And then I was hooked.

It was equal parts exciting, breathless, and confusing. The competitors had names like Djamolidine Abdoujaparov and Johan Museeuw. No-one else I knew took any interest. Those names contained far too many vowels. This was clearly the sport for me.

In 1994, on the streets of Lille for the Tour de France prologue, arrived British cyclist Chris Boardman.

He rolled down the ramp on his back-to-the-future bike (presumably having arrived earlier in a flying DeLorean) and scattered the world's finest time-trialists to the wind. Breaking records, claiming the Yellow Jersey, and giving me a new favourite sporting hero in my new favourite sport.

I couldn't wait to see him duking it out in the mountains with Pantani and denying Indurain a fourth successive Tour win.

I was all over this sport.

My optimism lasted two days.

The commentary team had been at pains to point out that Boardman was not there to win le Tour, that he was a TT specialist and not a Grand Tour contender, but I was a dreamer. New to all this, I though a good dose of British grit would see him right.

By day three he had all but disappeared from my TV screen.

I would spot him occasionally mid-peloton and wonder why he wasn't trying harder. Hadn't he already proved he was the fastest rider? Shouldn't he just ride off the front and away from them all?

My education had begun.

I quickly understood that this education included a compulsory module on the role of British cycling within the Tour de France, which could be summed up thus: any British cyclist will be either a niche specialist (Boardman); a workhorse team-player with the occasional moment of glory (Sean Yates); or an out of their depth no-hoper (naming no names).

Bit-part players to the main event of mahogany tanned Spaniards and flamboyant Italians.

Fast forward to the end of 2018. All three Grand Tours – the Giro d'Italia, the Tour de France, and the Vuelta Espana - are held by British cyclists. *Different* British cyclists. And riders from these islands have won six of the previous seven Tours de France (2012-2018).

Had Michael J. Fox appeared back in 1994 (in that DeLorean) and told me how the story of British cycling was going to pan out, I'd have laughed in his face. And also put a tenner on Wiggins for 2012, just to be on the safe side.

The seventeen-year-old me, of course, would've considered the 2018 iteration of pro cycling far too popular. Obvious. Unimaginative. I'd have avoided it to concentrate on something else. Something properly obscure. Pro windsurfing, perhaps, or competitive medieval re-enactment.

But I'd have been missing out. Those barren decades that preceded the British dominance were crucial; the context and the back story to the serial winning. The trough that makes the peak. And yet, it's not really even about the winning or the losing (ask me if I still feel this way when they're losing).

If a British cyclist fails to win a single race for the *next* twenty years I'll still be watching because of everything you've read in this book.

The drama, the nonsense, the trauma, the glory. The grey areas and the murky corners. This rich culture of style, etiquette, and pure athletic endeavour. Equal parts brilliant, ridiculous, honourable, and infuriating.

The truth is, I can still watch a bike race and wonder what on earth is going on. This is part of the appeal.

Why is that rider not attacking? Why is that guy's teammate eight minutes up the road? How come I haven't seen Mark Cavendish for nine days? Why, above all else, is that guy running, all clippy-cloppy up Mont Ventoux, as if his life depends on it?

Because he's a pro cyclist, and this is a Grand Tour, and thank God there are three more of these next year.

Printed in Great Britain
by Amazon

37743212R00123